Christian–Jewish Dialogue

Marcus Braybrooke

Christian–Jewish Dialogue

The Next Steps

scm press

0 334 02813 2

First published 2000
by SCM Press
9–17 St Albans Place, London N1 0NX

SCM Press is a division of
SCM-Canterbury Press Ltd

Typeset by Regent Typesetting, London
and printed in Great Britain by
Biddles Ltd, Guildford and King's Lynn

For
Elizabeth India Braybrooke
'a child of the new millennium'

'As Christians and Jews . . . we are called to be a blessing for the world. This is the common task awaiting us. It is therefore necessary for us, Christians and Jews, to be first a blessing to one another'

(Pope John Paul II on the 50th
anniversary of the uprising in the
Warsaw Ghetto, 6.4.1993)

CONTENTS

FOREWORD

Rabbi Joseph H. Ehrenkranz

Executive Director, Center for Christian–Jewish Understanding of Sacred Heart University, Fairfield, Connecticut

For the first time in two millennia, Jews and Christians have the opportunity to put aside their divisiveness and seek reconciliation and understanding. The twentieth century has seen unprecedented destruction and leaves us with choices for peace or war, hope or despair, forgiveness or revenge, faith or doubt and love or hate. A religious and moral memory is essential if we are to shape a future that will ensure mutual respect for all peoples and religions. In particular, the last half-century has seen dramatic changes in the ways that Christianity understands and interacts with Judaism. Christianity has been attempting to eliminate age-old prejudice and anti-Judaism, which has caused much suffering.

Certainly a major breakthrough in the journey between Jews and Christians was the decree of the Second Vatican Council, *Nostra Aetate* (1965), which was followed by other Vatican statements, notably the *Guidelines* (1974), the *Notes* (1985) and *We Remember: A Reflection on the Shoah* (1998). The writers of these documents affirmed the ongoing validity of the Jewish people who are not to be blamed for the death of Jesus. They also acknowledged the Christian share of responsibility for Jewish suffering throughout the centuries and stressed Jesus' solidarity with his people. There have been subsequent statements by many of the European and American Christian churches. Although these documents are not widely known, they are indeed, as Braybrooke says, 'like signposts marking the route that has been followed. They have had an influence in purging Christian liturgy and teaching of anti-Jewish material, but still too often Christian teaching is expounded by way of unfavourable contrast to Judaism' (p. 18). In short, we have come far in the last few decades to overcome past bitterness and have learned respectfully to share what we have seen and heard. But we have still far to go.

In his book *Christian–Jewish Dialogue: The Next Steps* Marcus Braybrooke, a scholar, teacher, pastor and friend, is unafraid to dialogue because he is convinced that the sharing of honest criticism and responses of friendship have made dialogue a pilgrimage of mutual respect that will lead to peace. Braybrooke does not point an accusing finger at the past relationship between Christians and Jews, but asks the reader to reflect on his or her own history. He challenges Jews and Christians to be a blessing to each other and to the world and challenges us to be committed to the essential task of interreligious dialogue for the sake of the growth and deeper self-understanding of Judaism and Christianity.

I am convinced that dialogue is the best path that can lead us forward in faith. At its best, dialogue is always a search for truth; it is not a matter of expedient political compromise or superficial religious negotiation. *Christian–Jewish Dialogue* neither attempts to accommodate beliefs by smoothing away the differences, nor does it engage in diplomatic evasions of the issues. Uneasy discussions of the implications of the Jewishness of Jesus, the teachings of Paul of Tarsus, triumphal attitudes and missionary efforts on the part of Christians towards Jews, the charge of deicide against the Jewish people, a more rigorous examination of how the Bible is read and interpreted in light of its place in history – especially the passion and resurrection narratives – and God's enduring covenant with the Jewish people are deftly handled with sensitivity, critical scholarship and faith. This is a book of scholarly research balanced with personal reflections by a pilgrim of peace who has 'walked the walk' and knows first-hand that the road to understanding is an uphill trek. His appropriate and timely political analogies and homiletic reflections seek to invite and encourage deeper respect and understanding between religions, particularly between Jews and Christians.

Braybrooke is correct that our relationship will deepen only when we are willing to dialogue about the experience that lies beneath our traditions, our most holy and intimate spiritual mysteries. And there are significant differences between Judaism and Christianity as well as intra-religious differences. Nonetheless, Jews and Christians are increasingly sharing in wider co-operative efforts. Further, there is a growing conviction that religions should work together for peace and justice. There will be no world peace without religious peace. Jews and Christians have become companions on the road of dialogue and understanding, with renewed hope for the cultivation of a world of peace for our children and grandchildren.

I am deeply grateful for this work because humanity's very survival depends on its ability to respect and share with each other the great wisdom contained in our religious traditions. The century which witnessed the horrors of the Shoah has also seen the growth of many enduring friendships between Jews and Christians. This is a sign that the deepest hatreds can be overcome by people of goodwill and faith. Now is the time for us to take the next steps in Christian–Jewish dialogue. Together we can confront the contemporary challenges that face us and I hope and pray that this extraordinary relationship of reconciliation will continue on the path of peace and justice which requires us to repair our wounded world.

PREFACE

I first visited Israel in 1958 and my first article to be published, in the mid-1960s, was on 'Anti-Semitism in the Fourth Gospel'. I have, therefore, thought, on and off, about many of the issues discussed in this book for nearly forty years. As a result, I owe a debt of gratitude to many people with whom I have talked about the questions of Christian–Jewish relations: to James Parkes, Bill Simpson, Peter Schneider, David Kessler, Edward Carpenter, George Appleton, Rabbi Hugo Gryn and many more.

I want particularly to record my thanks to Westminster College, Oxford – now the Westminster Institute of Education at Oxford Brookes University – for asking me to teach a course on Christian–Jewish relations and to the students for their comments and questions. I am grateful to many other organizations and groups, including the Council of Christians and Jews, the International Council of Christians and Jews, the Manor House Group, the Jewish–Christian–Muslim Dialogue Group of the Sternberg Centre, the Three Faiths Forum, the World Council of Churches' Consultation on the Church and the Jewish People, The Pastora Goldner Holocaust Symposium at Wroxton College, The Center for Christian–Jewish Understanding of Sacred Heart University, The Tantur Ecumenical Institute and other dialogue friends in Israel.

I owe a special debt of gratitude to John Bowden, as a friend, as a colleague in some of the dialogue groups and as a perceptive and encouraging editor, and to Margaret Lydamore for her work on this book. All who are interested in creative theological thinking owe an enormous debt to their work at SCM Press and it will be evident from the notes how much I have learned from books published by

SCM Press. I also want to thank Alex Wright, Anna Hardman and all the staff of SCM Press. Tony Bayfield has been a very special dialogue partner over the years and I am very grateful that he has written a response to this book and that Joseph Ehrenkranz has written a Foreword.

Once again, I express my thanks to my wife Mary for her support and encouragement, for the insights she has shared with me from her own active involvement in Christian–Jewish dialogue, and her very special gift for friendship.

That the century which saw the horrors of the Holocaust has also seen the blossoming of so many deep friendships between Jews and Christians is a message of hope that the deepest enmities can be overcome where people take the risk of being open to each other and to the mercy of God, who can free us from the bitter legacy of the past.

Marsh Baldon Rectory   Marcus Braybrooke
Passover and Easter 2000

INTRODUCTION

The last half-century has seen a dramatic change in Christians' understanding of Judaism and their attitude to the Jews. In large measure, this has been an attempt to eliminate the church's age-old prejudice and anti-Judaism, which has caused so much suffering, not least in contributing to the Holocaust.

The changes, however, are still not widely enough known and their relevance to the life of the whole church little considered. They are not just of interest to those with a special concern for Christian–Jewish relations. A proper understanding of Judaism and the church's relation to the Jewish people is relevant to large parts of the church's theology and preaching, because God's covenant in Jesus Christ is inextricably linked to God's covenant with the children of Israel. Thinking through the theological implications of the new approach to Judaism is significant for the renewal of the church and is also an essential preliminary to further progress in Christian–Jewish co-operation.

This book, therefore, suggests first that the reluctance of the churches to engage in this theological rethinking and to recognize the consequences of seeing the Jewish people as still the people of God is a major reason why Christian–Jewish dialogue has got bogged down. There is then a brief survey of the progress made in Christian–Jewish relations in the twentieth century. The theological discussion concentrates on aspects of the New Testament. It deals first with Jesus' relation to the Judaism of his day, which is now seen to be very varied. Jesus was a faithful Jew. The fact that he had sharp disagreements with some of his contemporaries does not imply that he was opposed to Judaism. The debates were internal Jewish arguments. The record of Jesus' ministry should not be read as a Christian argument against Judaism, but as highlighting discussion about the obedience that God requires – a discussion that cuts across religious divides.

Equally, discussion of the death of Jesus should not be about *who* killed Jesus – although it is still important to stop blame being falsely placed on 'the Jews' – but about *what* killed Jesus. The passion narrative highlights human greed, corruption and evil, which are still too evident in the world. In the same way, the resurrection of Jesus should not be used by preachers to prove that Christianity is right. A careful reading of the Gospel records emphasizes the mystery of what happened and that the Risen Christ was only known to those with faith. Belief in the resurrection is not a conviction about an observable external event but commitment in hope to the way of Jesus.

A new understanding of Judaism also makes clear that the first Jews who believed in Jesus did not think they were joining a new religion. It was only when the church became predominantly Gentile and adopted Hellenistic ways of thought that christological and trinitarian doctrines developed that created an unbridgeable gap between the two religions. It may be that Christians need to go back to the thinking of the New Testament, not only to heal centuries of anti-Judaism and Christian triumphalism, but to make sense for today of the conviction that God was in Christ.

Equally, a new approach to Paul suggests that he did not reject the Jewish Law as such, but only its application to Gentile converts to the church. Equally, the covenant relationship with God now available to Gentiles in Christ did not replace God's covenant relationship with the Jewish people. Until the church, however, really accepts that Jews are a people of God and abandons missionary efforts to convert Jews, there will continue to be an uneasy relationship. Indeed, God's presence needs to be recognized not only in Judaism, but in all the great world religions. This recognition is essential if Jews and Christians and all people of faith are gladly to work together for the healing of the world.

For the church theologically to interiorize the new understanding of Judaism expressed in official documents is, therefore, of great importance to the renewal of the church's life and thinking, to its relations with people of other faiths and to its service to the world.

I have tried to write in a way that does not require the reader to have a training in theology, while providing in the notes sufficient references for the student to pursue the subject further.

1

THE PRESENT PLATEAU

Christian–Jewish dialogue has got stuck. I am not alone in thinking this. Rabbi David Rosen, the former Chief Rabbi of Ireland who now works in Israel, has said there is a sense of 'treading water'.[1] The *Journal of Ecumenical Studies* 1997 summer issue contained a number of articles on Jewish–Christian relations under the heading 'The Unfinished Agenda'. The picture I prefer is of climbers making their way up a mountain. As you come near to what from below appears to be the top, you suddenly find there are other higher peaks which beckon you on. Christians and Jews have climbed a long way in the last fifty years but they seem to have reached a plateau. There are further tasks that lie ahead.

This is in no way to minimize the great achievements of the last fifty years. Gerald Priestland, a former BBC Correspondent on Religious Affairs, once said that the change in Christian–Jewish relations was one of the few pieces of good religious news in recent years.

There are various reasons why Christian–Jewish dialogue may have got stuck. Some are to do with the internal life of each religion and some to do with the relationship between the two faiths.

It is probably fair to say that both religions have other apparently more pressing problems. Both, at least in Europe and North America, are suffering a numerical decline. For Jews, this is in part because of the growing number of Jews who 'marry out', that is to say who marry a Gentile. A Jew has to be born of a Jewish mother, so if a Jewish man marries a non-Jewish woman, the children are not Jewish.[2] Even if a Jewish woman marries a Gentile man and the children count as Jewish, it may be difficult to maintain a Jewish home and to give the children a sense of Jewish identity. The question Jews often ask themselves is 'Will we have Jewish grand-children?'

There has also perhaps been some lessening of the ties which bind the Jewish community together. The Holocaust remains a defining event for the contemporary Jewish world and the memory must not be allowed to fade. Yet the number of survivors of the death camps declines each year. The children of survivors have their own emotional legacy to bear, but with the passing of time, the future of Jewish life – shaped of course by the past – becomes a more vital concern. The so-called six hundred and fourteenth *mitzvah* not to let Hitler win a posthumous victory becomes less compelling. Israel's security also seems more assured than twenty years ago. Admittedly, the peace process in Israel/Palestine only just avoids grinding to a halt, but at least the defence of Israel is not as urgent a priority for the Diaspora as it was to a previous generation. No longer also do Jews in the West have to campaign for their fellow Jews behind the Iron-Curtain, even though anti-Semitism is still in evidence in Eastern Europe.

Several studies have suggested that identification with the Jewish people, particularly as a protest against the Holocaust and anti-Semitism and as a gesture of support for Israel and Soviet Jews, has been a more important reason in recent years for synagogue membership than personal commitment to the God of Israel. As the reasons for such identification become less compelling – and they were ones which united Jews in self-defence against a hostile world – so attachment to Jewish life may weaken.

Jonathan Sacks, Chief Rabbi of Great Britain and the Common-wealth, has written:

> Physical survival has dominated modern Jewish concern, and that it why the Holocaust and the State of Israel have been central to Jewish thought. The Holocaust stands as the symbol of the risk Jews face. Israel stands as the guarantor of Jewish lives and liberties worldwide. But physical survival is not the problem con-fronting most Diaspora Jewries. It is not seriously endangered in either America or Britain. What is at risk is neither life nor liberty

but identity. The question is not 'Will we survive?' but '*How* will we survive?' As Jews? Or as something else, whose Jewish content will rapidly diffuse through the generations until nothing of it remains?[3]

Further, there are serious divisions within the Jewish world between the Orthodox and Progressive traditions. There are also tensions within Orthodoxy between the so-called 'ultra-Orthodox' and the 'middle of the way' traditional Jews. These divisions vary from country to country but inevitably absorb energy which might otherwise have been used to address the non-Jewish world.

In the Christian world, there are also deep divisions, despite the ecumenical movement. At the 1998 Assembly of the World Council of Churches held in Harare, George Carey, Archbishop of Canterbury, asked in a sermon: 'Are we going to seek unity in the service of Christ's mission for the world, or sink under the weight of division, controversy and suspicion?'[4] The Orthodox churches feel marginalized in the World Council of Churches and the Roman Catholic Church is not a member. Divisions today are, however, not so much between different denominations but within each denomination between the so-called 'liberals' and 'conservatives'. As a self-confessed liberal, I have to admit that the conservatives seem to be in the ascendancy. So, because 'progressive' Jews and 'liberal' Christians take the lead in maintaining dialogue, it only has limited influence in either community.

To many in the world church, Christian–Jewish dialogue seems a particular concern of European and North American churches. It is sometimes implied that it is only European Christians who have to deal with their sense of guilt for the Holocaust.[5] Recent years have seen, in both the Catholic and Protestant world, a steady growth in the numbers and influence of African, Asian and Latin American Christians, many of whom, except in Latin America, have no direct contact with Jewish people. Although the relationship with Judaism and the Jewish people is relevant to all Christians, this is certainly not self-evident. In Africa, relationships with Islam are far more pressing. It is also true that in recent years Christians from Africa and Asia have been likely to identify with the Palestinians against the Israelis, whom they see as latter-day Western imperialists. This has meant that the World Council of Churches has been reluctant to bring theological concerns about the relationship of Jews and Christians to an Assembly lest the discussion is high-jacked by those who want the World Council of Churches to speak out in support of the Palestinians.

One of the tasks which still lies ahead, therefore, is to make far more widely known in churches and synagogues the import-ant post-war advances in Christian–Jewish relationships. I was reminded of this recently, when I was asked to advise on a fairly popular book about the New Testament. The account of the trial of Jesus put the blame for the death of Jesus clearly on to the Jewish leaders and people. Those fateful words from Matthew, 'His blood be on us and on our children!' (Matt. 27.25) were quoted. The author's response when I suggested that this was unacceptable was, 'But that is what the New Testament says.' Many Christians still assume that the Gospels are eye-witness accounts of the ministry of Jesus. There is a prior task of helping Christians to appreciate an out-line of modern New Testament studies even before they can be helped to see that traditional attitudes to the Jews are wrong.

That, however, is not why Christian–Jewish dialogue is stuck, because that is a matter of telling people how far we have climbed. The reason the dialogue is bogged down is because of a reluctance to grapple with the theological issues that arise for members of both faiths because of our new understanding of the Jewish–Christian relationship.

Shaye J. D. Cohen, Professor of Judaic Studies at Brown University, says that the fundamental issue on the agenda can be reduced to a single phrase: 'to work out a theology of the other'. 'It is not enough simply to believe in tolerance, not enough simply to allow the other's existence,' he explains, 'rather, what we need is a theology on each side to validate the other's existence.'[6] For example, he suggests Jews should try to answer the question, 'How is the divine cause somehow advanced by having millions and millions of Christians in the world?'[7] In a similar way, Shaye Cohen wants Christians to answer the question, 'Why are the Jews still here?'[8]

An important task ahead is to make room in our theologies for the 'other' as people or servants of God – whereas for centuries Christians have seen all who are not of the true faith or indeed not of the true church as enemies of God.[9]

Many Christians have abandoned that position. Statements from a number of churches recognize that God's covenant with the Jewish people is still valid,[10] but there is a lot of theological rethinking to be done. Allan Brockway, then on the staff of the World Council of Churches, wrote ten years ago: 'Those churches which incorporate the continuing reality of the covenant between the Jewish people and God into their official theology establish a premise with far-reaching implications, both for their relations with the Jewish people and for Christian theology.' He added that 'By and large the development and implementation of those implications remain in the future.'[11] For Christians to recognize that God's covenant with the Jewish people is still valid is to have to modify traditional exclusive claims to the truth and the assumption that they have a monopoly on salvation. More immediately, not only attempts to convert Jews are called in question but traditional claims that Jesus is unique and perhaps how the church has traditionally understood his divinity. This in turn opens up the question of the relation of Christianity not only to Judaism but to other world religions.

That is challenging enough, but to take the 'other' seriously also requires us to look again at the ministry, death and resurrection of Jesus Christ. It has become quite common for New Testament scholars to acknowledge that Jesus was a faithful Jew rather than a critic of all things Jewish who came to found a new religion. This suggests that the polemic in the Gospels dates to the time when they were written and not to the ministry of Jesus himself. Yet this is an unstable basis for a new relationship between Jews and Christians, as scholarly fashions can change. Rather the arguments between Jesus and some of his contemporaries illustrate different ways of responding to God's will. It is a question of 'What doth the Lord require?', not Judaism versus Christianity. Equally, discussion of the passion –

in so far as the historical facts can be unravelled – should not be a question of who killed Jesus but *what* killed Jesus. The passion highlights the complexity of human motivation and what faithfulness to God requires. Just as the death of Jesus must not be blamed on the Jewish people, so his resurrection should not be treated as an objective event which proved that he was right. The resurrection should be proclaimed as a commitment in hope to follow the way of Jesus. All the Gospel material is coloured by the concerns of the early Christian community. The recognition that the partings of the ways was as much for historical reasons as for theological throws open the question whether Christians are for ever bound to tread the path mapped out by the church in the early centuries. If you are lost, it may be good to go back and start out on another track. This is particularly the case with christology because the creeds, shaped by Greek philosophy, distort the New Testament witness to Jesus in a way which has increased the gap between Christians and Jews and Muslims.

Christians are so used to looking to the New Testament as the writings that define their faith that they approach them with a deeply held expectation that they are there to confirm what they believe. But perhaps taking the other seriously should encourage us to recognize that the different choices made by those who did and who did not follow Jesus were genuine choices made with equally serious motivation. This will allow us to see that the various positions taken illuminate contemporary struggles of people of faith to obey God in the world today.

This book then is primarily a Christian reflection on the New Testament by a Christian who is trying to take the other seriously. I have long been challenged by words of the German theologian, Friedrich-Wilhelm Marquardt, who said, 'We will only have Christian anti-Judaism behind us when theologically we will have succeeded in making positive sense of the Jewish "no" to Jesus.'[12] Only then, will Jews and Christians be freed from the legacy of the past to work together with people of all faiths in our common calling to share in the healing of the world.

2

LOOKING BACK

A plateau is a place to pause and recoup one's strength before moving on. It is legitimate, therefore, to take a few pages to look back to see how Jewish–Christian dialogue has developed in the twentieth century.

It is hard to recall how much one knew about a subject before one started to know anything about it – if that makes sense! A visit to Israel in 1958, while I was doing my National Service in Cyprus, introduced me not only to the Land of Jesus, but to the vibrant new Israeli nation. From our Jewish guide, who was always armed, I caught something of the enthusiasm of Israel's citizens and learned of the new nation's struggle to survive. A visit to West Jerusalem – East Jerusalem was then under Jordanian control – included time at the Chamber of the Holocaust on Mount Zion. (Yad Vashem had not then been built.) I vividly remember my appalled horror at seeing the bars of soap made out of human corpses and other relics of the atrocities. My father had served in the army and had spoken a little about the war, but I do not recall him talking about the death camps. Indeed, at that time few people wished to recall those horrors. Even in 1961 the Council of Christians and Jews (CCJ) did not wish to associate itself with an exhibition about the concentration camps which was being staged in Coventry. It was felt that the exhibition was likely to perpetuate hatred and bitterness.[1]

As Rosemary Radford Ruether, an American scholar who has made a big contribution to Christian–Jewish study has said, 'It took more than two decades for theological reflection on the Shoah to begin to be articulated and for Jews and some Christians to recognize that theological business could not continue after this fissure had opened up in the world.'[2]

Thinking back to my school days, one of my teachers had been a prisoner of war, but I do not remember him speaking about the extermination of the Jews. I studied modern European history to 'A' level, but I do not recall that the Jews were part of that history – admittedly 'modern history' ended at 1914! I recollect that someone said that one of the house masters was a Jew (his name was Jacobs, but that did not signify!), but he did not seem to have any difficulty with 'public school religion'. I do not recall that at church there was any overtly anti-Jewish teaching. Those involved in the passion of Our Lord were seen to represent the evil behaviour to which we all are tempted. At university I became aware of the Council of Christians and Jews (CCJ), which at that time had its summer conference in Cambridge and I began to meet some Jews who were concerned for dialogue with Christians. It was a rude shock twenty years later when I joined the staff of CCJ to find that many Jews were not keen on such dialogue – neither were a number of Christians!

There can be no doubt about the church's long history of anti-Jewish teaching, but the point of my reminiscences is to encourage you to reflect on your own history. Where do we, each one of us, join the journey in search of a new relationship of Christians and Jews? I have met some German Christians and a few British Christians who recall being taught in Sunday school that the Jews were to blame for the death of Jesus. Any churchgoer would have heard those fateful words, 'His blood be on us and on our children!' But many Christians today have been spared the full horror of the church's traditional anti-Jewish teaching and if, as it were, they have come by cable car to the point up the mountain which we have now reached, they will not know how much effort has gone into arriving at this plateau.

The traditional view was that Jesus came as God's Son to found the church. The Jews failed to recognize that he was the long-promised Messiah and plotted to have him put to death. Thereby the Jews forfeited the promises which had been made to them in the *Old* Covenant and were banished from the land of Israel. These promises were taken over by the church, the *new* Israel, which lived by grace and not the Law. Often Christians spoke of Jews as 'children of the devil' (cf. John 8.44). Infamous libels were invented about the Jews, who were made to wear distinctive dress and forced to live in ghettos. Of course, the plight of Jews varied from country to country and from century to century and a distinction needs to be made between the official teaching of the church and popular prejudice. At times, as for a period in medieval Spain, there was creative inter-action between members of the two faiths, but on the whole Christendom's treatment of the Jews was degrading and a matter of shame, and Christian anti-Judaism is recognized as one major cause of the Holocaust.[3]

In the nineteenth century there were some important changes to Jewish life. A growing number of Jews migrated from Eastern Europe to Western Europe and North America. As they did so, they came out of the ghetto and to varying degrees were allowed to share in civic and public life without discrimination. Many Jews made a remarkable contribution to European thought and culture. Emancipation, however, brought new questions about how Jews should relate to the wider Gentile society. Some Jews converted to Christianity, others assimilated. Divisions also took place within the Jewish world with the emergence of Reform Judaism.

There was also renewed hostility. In the late nineteenth century, pogroms in Russia, and growing anti-Semitism in Western Europe, which some politicians exploited, were warnings of the dangers to come. Some Jews believed that the only lasting security for their people was the creation of a Zionist state. In the churches, there was a new missionary concern for the conversion of the Jews. To the Jews this was as threatening as anti-Semitism, but it also occasioned among some Christians a new interest in Judaism. Critical study of the Bible also meant that some scholars were beginning to ask new questions about the scriptures.

It has been said of the late nineteenth and early twentieth centuries that Jews and Christians 'engaged not in dialogue but in double monologue. Christians wanted to prove the superiority of their faith; Jews were primarily concerned with bettering their lot in society. Christians wanted converts; Jews, civil rights. Jews were forced to talk religion where they meant social betterment.'⁴

The beginnings of change

Rosenzweig and Buber

In the early years of this century, the situation slowly began to change. A few seminal Jewish scholars, especially Hermann Cohen, Franz Rosenzweig and Martin Buber expressed a new interest in Christianity. Hermann Cohen (1842–1918), a philosopher who brought a new interpretation to the thought of Immanuel Kant, was a professor at Marburg from 1876 to 1912. Cohen, in response to an attack on the Jews for lack of patriotism made by the historian Treitschke in 1879, maintained that German Jews were completely loyal to German society, while practising their own religion. He argued that as God's chosen people they had a particular duty to bring about the unity of humanity and to establish God's kingdom on earth. He argued that observance of the Sabbath was the first step towards the abolition of slavery. His best known book, *The Religion of Reason from the Sources of Judaism* (1919), was published a year after his death. Cohen wrote extensive critiques of Christianity, but he had a sense of the deep relationship between Judaism and Christianity, especially in its Protestant manifestations.

Franz Rosenzweig (1886–1929) was born into an assimilated family. As a young man he considered converting to Christianity, but in 1913, after attending a High Holy Day service, he resolved to remain faithful to Judaism. While still a soldier in the First World War, he wrote *The Star of Redemption*. Rosenzweig held that there are two valid religions of revelation, Judaism and Christianity. As Ronald Miller puts it:

> Rosenzweig asserts that what is finally and convincingly real for the Jew is God and God's (ultimate) kingdom; but what grasps the Christian as most real is Christ and the interim kingdom, this present course of sacred history. This constitutes an irreconcilable difference in their articulated faith and their spirituality.

And yet both religions are a part of God's salvational plan and providence; both covenantal communities grasp a reality which has the power of eliciting a life and death loyalty, i.e both are not only true but real religions.[5]

In his correspondence with his cousin Hans Ehrenberg, who spoke of his 'Christian Judaism', Rosenzweig asked, 'What is your reality, the basis on which you operate? Jesus or God? If you hold that Jesus is the Messiah and know yourself to belong to the interim kingdom, then God is just truth for you and Jesus alone is a reality. And then you are simply a Christian, without any modifiers. For me, only God is a reality'.[6]

Martin Buber (1878–1965), best known for his book *I and Thou* (1923), which emphasizes the distinctive quality of personal relationships, also accepted the reality of Christianity as a path to God and asked Christians to say the same of Judaism. He spoke of Jesus as 'my brother' and saw in both religions a similar commitment to suffering and prophetic service.

Other Jewish scholars, such as Claude Montefiore, a Liberal Jew, and Joseph Klausner, who was an unsuccessful candidate to be the first president of Israel, began to study Jesus and Paul.

Christian scholars

At the same time, some Christian scholars were beginning a slow but vital reassessment of Judaism. It is worth emphasizing their work, as sometimes it is suggested that the more favourable view now taken of the Pharisees by many New Testament scholars is out of a desire, after the Holocaust, for better relations with the Jewish people. This may be a consequence of such work, but scholarly work should be independent of such external motivation. Rather, scholarly study of Jewish sources has shown that traditional Christian pictures of the Pharisees and rabbinical Judaism are wrong. The pioneers were Robert Travers Herford (1860–1950) and George Foot Moore (1851–1931). Robert Travers Herford was a Unitarian minister and scholar, whose many works on the Talmud and Midrash helped to begin a proper Christian appreciation of Rabbinical Judaism and a new less jaundiced view of the Pharisees. The greatest work of George Foot Moore (1851–1931) of Harvard University was his three-volume *Judaism in the First Centuries of the Christian Era*, published between 1927 and 1930.

Another pioneer, who exposed the Christian roots of anti-Semitism, was James Parkes (1896–1981), an Anglican clergyman, who in 1928 went to Geneva to take charge of the International Student Service of the Student Christian Movement (SCM). He soon became aware of the rising tide of anti-Semitism on the continent of Europe. As early as 1930, he rejected a missionary approach to the Jews. Writing to Conrad Hoffmann, who had been appointed director of the recently formed International Committee on the Christian Approach to the Jews, Parkes said: 'We are, quite definitely, not interested in the evangelization of the individual Jew. It seems to me that your brethren have completely left out of account another alternative, which seems to me to be the most truly Christian one at the present time: our Christian responsibility to give the Jew a square deal to be a Jew.'[7] Parkes came to insist on the theological equality of the revelation of Sinai and of the incarnation. In 1934 his doctoral thesis 'The Conflict of the Church and the Synagogue: A Study in the Origins of anti-Semitism' was published. Parkes was clear that Christianity and Christian theologians were to blame for the unique evil of anti-Semitism. 'The central and overpowering, indeed horrifying conclusion, which that research brought me,' he wrote, 'was the total responsibility of the Christian Church for turning a normal xenophobia (fear of foreigners) into the unique disease of anti-Semitism.'[8] A prolific writer, Parkes devoted his life to promoting a new Christian appreciation of Judaism.

Besides the work of pioneering scholars, a few Christians and Jews were beginning to meet for friendly discussion, for example in Britain under the auspices of the London Society for the Study of Religions, the World Congress of Faiths and especially the (London) Society of Jews and Christians. In the USA, the origins of National Conference of Christians and Jews (now the National Conference) go back to the 1920s.

The Second World War and its aftermath in the churches

By the mid-1930s, with the rise to power of the Nazis in Germany, the more practical issues of helping refugees and combating anti-Semitism were becoming uppermost. The outbreak of war and the further deterioration of the situation led in Britain to the formation of the Council of Christians and Jews to combat all forms of religious and racial intolerance and to promote goodwill between Christians and Jews.

The opening of the concentration camps, with the appalling evidence of the bestial treatment of the Jews by the Nazis, and then the creation of the state of Israel, gave a new urgency to the search for better Christian–Jewish relations, but at first developments were slow. In an important book, *The Teaching of Contempt* (1956), the French Jewish historian, Jules Isaac, by a thorough study of Christian scripture and the writings of the church fathers, made clear the link between Christian theology and anti-Semitism.

A major breakthrough was the decree of the Second Vatican Council, *Nostra Aetate* (1965), which was followed by the Vatican documents *Guidelines* (1974) and *Notes* (1985). Similar documents have been agreed by many other churches, although the Orthodox Church has been slow to accept this new approach.[10] In addition to church statements, there have been a series of regular meetings of representatives of the Jewish world with representatives of the Roman Catholic Church and of the World Council of Churches, as well as a the great variety of unofficial dialogue groups. It should also be mentioned that the Vatican's recognition of the state of Israel in 1993 removed a further cause of friction.

Looking back after twenty years, Gerhard Riegner, who for many years was Secretary General of the World Jewish Congress and an active participant in dialogue, summed up the eight major principles that *Nostra Aetate* established like this:

1. The declaration stresses the spiritual bond between the Church and the Jewish people.
2. It acknowledges that it received the 'Old Testament through the people with whom God concluded the Ancient Covenant'.

3. It acknowledges the Judaic roots of Christianity, starting with the Jewish origin of Jesus himself, of the Virgin Mary and of all the Apostles.

4. It declares that God does not repent of the gifts he makes and the calls he issues and that Jews remain 'most dear to God'.

5. It states that what happened in the Passion of Christ cannot be charged against all Jews without distinction then living, nor against Jews of today.

6. It declares that the Jews are not rejected or accursed by God.

7. It proclaims the Church's repudiation of hatred, persecution, and displays of anti-Semitism at any time by anyone.

8. It fosters and recommends mutual understanding and respect through biblical and theological studies and fraternal dialogues.

It may be helpful to put alongside this summary the statement of the World Council of Churches Consultation on the Church and the Jewish People (WCC:CCJP) issued after the group's meeting at Sigtuna in Sweden in 1988. The statement suggested that there was wide agreement among the member Churches of the World Council of Churches that:

1. The covenant of God with the Jewish people remains valid. It had not been replaced by God's new covenant with the church.

2. Anti-Semitism and all forms of the teaching of contempt for Judaism, especially teaching about deicide, are to be repudiated.

3. The living tradition of Judaism is a gift of God.

4. Coercive proselytism directed towards Jews is incompatible with Christian faith.

5. Jews and Christians bear a common responsibility as witnesses to God's righteousness and peace in the world.

The group recognized that the Jewish people are not to be blamed for the death of Jesus. They acknowledged the Christian share of responsibility for Jewish sufferings through the centuries. They also stressed Jesus' solidarity with his people.

Similar teaching has been expressed in the statements of many of the European and American member churches of the World Council of Churches. Even though few members of the churches are familiar with these documents and statements, they are like signposts marking the route that has been followed. They have had an influence in purging Christian liturgy and teaching of anti-Jewish material, but still too often Christian teaching is expounded by way of unfavourable contrast to Judaism.

3

THE JEWISH WORLD AT THE TIME OF JESUS

'Jesus was and always remained a Jew.'[1] A dramatic change in how Jesus is seen to relate to the Judaism of his day is central to the new Christian approach to Judaism.[2] Jesus is now often spoken of as 'a faithful Jew', rather than as a determined critic of all things Jewish. It is suggested that he did not intend to found a new religion. Rather, the break between church and synagogue happened gradually in the latter part of the first century CE.[3] Further, the Jews are not to be blamed for the death of Jesus. Responsibility for his crucifixion is placed squarely on the Roman governor Pilate and his soldiers.

The fact of Jesus' Jewishness has seldom actually been denied, except by some Christians with Nazi sympathies, but very often it was forgotten – as is shown by many of the pictures of Jesus painted through the centuries by Western European artists.[4] It was a surprise to many of his readers, therefore, when early in the twentieth century the biblical scholar Julius Wellhausen (1844–1918) wrote, 'Jesus was not a Christian but a Jew.'[5]

The importance of this was brought home to me in a discussion with Eberhard Bethge, a close friend of Dietrich Bonhoeffer and editor of his *Ethics* and *Letters and Papers from Prison*. I expressed unease about saying Jesus was 'the Jewish Messiah', because it is clear that there were different Jewish expectations about the Messiah and that Jesus did not fit with these. It was wrong, therefore, to blame the Jews for not recognizing 'their' Messiah, as happens, for example, in this verse from a popular Advent hymn:

Every eye shall now behold him
Robed in dreadful majesty;
Those who set at nought and sold him,
Pierced and nailed him to the tree,
Deeply wailing,
Shall the true Messiah see.[6]

In reply Eberhard Bethge reminded me that in the context of Nazi
Germany it was a very significant and dangerous remark to say that
'Jesus was the Jewish Messiah.' It was a way of affirming the indis-
soluble link between the Christian church and the Jewish people.
Indeed in his *Ethics*, Bonhoeffer wrote:

Jesus Christ was the promised Messiah of the Israelite-Jewish
people, and for that reason the line of our forefathers goes back
beyond the appearance of Jesus Christ to the people of Israel.
Western history is, by God's will, indissolubly linked with
the people of Israel, not only genetically but also in genuine
uninterrupted encounter. The Jew keeps open the question
of Christ. He is the sign of the free mercy-choice and of the
repudiating wrath of God. 'Behold therefore the goodness and
severity of God' (Rom. 11.22). An expulsion of the Jews from the
West must necessarily bring with it the expulsion of Christ. For
Jesus Christ was a Jew.[7]

The new picture of Jesus as a faithful Jew seems, at least at first sight,
to be at odds with the Gospels. Rooting out the anti-Judaism of
Christian teaching demands a critical reading of the Gospels, but
this is something many Christians shy away from. There is a need
for a more rigorous examination of how the Bible is read and interpreted in the church – but that is another discussion.

The attempt to give a historical reconstruction of the life and
ministry of Jesus has occupied scholars for over a century and a half.
Even so, there are few agreed conclusions and some people have
wondered whether it is a quest for a mirage.

Part of the difficulty is great uncertainty about the historical
reliability of our sources of information about both Jesus and first-
century Jewish religious life.

The sources

The problem with the material about first-century Judaism is that much of it dates from a later period. Rabbinic Judaism was codified from the second century CE. Many rabbinic debates reflect the new situation which existed after the destruction of Jerusalem and the Temple in the year 70 CE when Judaism had to adapt to a totally new situation. So, although in the 1970s and 1980s several scholars showed that the New Testament picture of the Pharisees was unfair,[9] today there is more uncertainty whether one can use rabbinic material as evidence of the teachings and practices of the Pharisees.[10]

Another source is the Jewish historian Josephus. For the history of Hasmonean rule up to the death of Herod the Great, he used detailed information from Nicolaus of Damascus, who was a secretary to Herod the Great. His information about the next thirty years is skimpy; thereafter the accounts become fuller, although we seldom know his sources. His reliability is open to question, particularly because during the Jewish Revolt, he went over to the Romans.[11]

Because of the discovery of the Dead Sea Scrolls and other material, we know that Judaism in the first century CE was far more varied than is suggested by the Gospels or the Jewish historian. The provenance and interpretation of these new sources has been hotly debated.[12]

The situation is no better with the Gospels.[13] It is now widely recognized that the Gospels are not straightforward historical accounts of the life of Jesus, but are influenced by the concerns of the early Christian community.

Unravelling the evidence about Jesus and seeing him in a Jewish milieu is, therefore, complex. Our knowledge of Jesus is mediated by the early Christian community, which in the light of the resurrection believed him to be God's 'Anointed One' (Acts 4.27). The Gospels reflect these beliefs and also Christian polemic against Jews who did not believe in Jesus. It is generally agreed that the earliest Gospel, Mark, was written about thirty years or more after the death of Jesus. Luke and Matthew were perhaps written at least ten years later, although they used material from Mark. By the time they were written, Jerusalem had fallen to the Romans (70 CE) and the acrimony between those Jews who did and those who did not believe in Jesus was intense.[14] The Jewish Christian community had fled to Pella in Perea before Jerusalem fell – probably between 66–68 CE. Their 'desertion' alienated other Jews. Further, by leaving Jerusalem, their ties with the Temple and the rest of the Jewish community were weakened. About the same time believers in Jesus 'were put out of the synagogue' (John 9.22). This is reflected in the Fourth Gospel, where the term 'Jews' is used of the opponents of Jesus, even though some at least of the Johannine community were Jewish believers in Jesus.[15]

All the Gospels, therefore, reflect the bitter disputes that were taking place at the time they were written between members of the early church and many Jews . They do not give an accurate picture of events during Jesus' ministry or his relation to the very varied Judaism of his day. Even before the material in the Gospels was written down, it had circulated orally in the Christian community for some thirty years. During this time it had been shaped by its use in worship, teaching and preaching. The authenticity of any saying attributed to Jesus is, therefore, open to question.[16] Any reconstruction of his life and ministry has to be pursued with great caution and hesitancy.

First-century Judaism

What do we know of the religious scene at the time of Jesus? Josephus speaks of three religious parties: The Pharisees, the Sadducees and the Essenes.

The Pharisees

In Josephus the Pharisees appear in the early first century CE as political opponents of the ruling Hasmoneans, although they had at first allied with them. They were probably connected with the 'Hasidim', 'the pious ones', who were originally allied with the Maccabees (I Macc. 2.42). Both groups were concerned that the

Temple should be cleansed and rededicated after it had been defiled by the Hellenistic ruler Antiochus in 168 BCE, but the Hasidim were sceptical about a purely military and political development of power. Some of them may have been executed by Alexander Jannaeus, although they gained favour under Queen Alexandra Salome (76–67) and at that time may have gained some representation on the Sanhedrin. Under Herod, according to some scholars, such as Jacob Neusner, the Pharisees withdrew from political life and became more concerned for spiritual matters, as the development of the schools of Hillel and Shammai may suggest. Martin Hengel, however, argues that private life was the only free space which a subject people have. Pharisees seem to have been linked with the resistance led by Judas of Galilee. The extent of their influence is also debated. Hengel argues that the Pharisees decisively shaped first-century Judaism, whereas E. P. Sanders suggests that the priests in Jerusalem were the dominant religious influence at the time.[17]

The Hebrew word *perushim*, which may mean someone who distinguishes precisely, fits Josephus' description of the Pharisees. It may have been a term applied to them in a derogatory sense by opponents and the Pharisees may be the community of the Liar in the Qur'an texts.

Although the origins of the Pharisaic movement are uncertain, by the end of the Maccabean period, in the first century BCE, they were bringing about a far-reaching change in Judaism, which has had a continuing influence up to the present day. The Pharisees had a new perception of the relationship of God to human beings. God was not just the God of the patriarchs nor just the parent of Israel, but the God of every individual. God watched over and cared for each person. New names were given to God, such as Makom, 'the all present', Ha-Kadosh Baruch Hu, 'The Holy One Blessed be He', or Abinu She-Bashamayim, 'Our Father who art in heaven'.

As a direct result of the new understanding of the God–human relationship, the Pharisees taught belief in the resurrection – a teaching which brought them into conflict with the Sadducees, who were the high priestly party. It was among the Pharisees that the position of rabbi, or teacher, emerged. They also developed the synagogue, as a place for communal assembly. While not opposing the Temple ritual, they gave a symbolic interpretation to the sacrifices and insisted that they had no efficacy apart from genuine repentance and reparation.

The Pharisees' teaching about the covenant and Torah was true to the biblical teaching. They called for obedience in response to God's mercy. Pharisaism, which was a lay movement, took seriously the obligation laid upon Israel as a whole to be 'a holy nation' before God. Purity was not just for priests at the Temple, but for all God's people. Taking the call to holiness seriously, the Pharisees sought to apply the Law to contemporary life and here disagreed with the Sadducees, the high priestly party, who stuck to a literal and often out-of-date interpretation.

The Torah was the major source of information on ordering the cult – the Temple worship – but it also showed the way of life that God expected. It was, however, seldom precise enough to show the exact behaviour required, while, of course, life changes and laws have to be reapplied to new circumstances. There therefore grew up a cumulative reinterpretation and application of Torah. Some of it was based on interpretation of a passage of scripture; some of it took the form of a pronouncement by a rabbi and in addition there are stories which illustrate the teaching. In interpreting the Law, the Pharisees were guided by two principles. One was to build a fence around the Torah; the other was to make explicit what was implicit or unsaid. John Bowker of Cambridge University, who has made a particular study of rabbinic material, suggests that 'the people welcomed the assistance of the Hakamim (the learned) in alleviating the strictest interpretation of Torah and in defending their traditional ways'.[18]

The Pharisees also stressed table fellowship (haburah). To belong to a fellowship a person had to undertake certain obligations of purity and a disciplined way of life. The aim was to regard the whole world, not just the Temple, as a sanctuary where God dwells. Inevitably these rules separated the Pharisees from ordinary people, in the way Masons or vegetarians may separate themselves. There is no evidence, however, that they expected everyone to obey those self-chosen rules nor that they thought the common people were excluded from salvation. The picture that some Christians have of the Pharisees as an exclusive group looking down on others is not supported by the evidence. The 'sinners' with whom Jesus mixed were not the common people, but criminals and collaborators with the Roman occupying power.

Jesus' arguments with the Pharisees, as reported in the Gospels, were no greater that the arguments among the Pharisees. Just as there were sharp differences among the rabbis, for example, between Hillel and Shammai, so it seems there were also sharp differences among the Pharisees. Yet, 'more important than the divisions were the far greater unities of methods, beliefs and intentions which they held in common, and which differentiated them as a whole from, for example, the Sadducees or the communities on the shore of the Dead Sea'.[19]

It seems that the Pharisees were concerned – some perhaps excessively – about purity or cleanness and about tithes and festivals. Neusner suggests that this is indicated by rabbinic material which can be dated to before 70 CE. Josephus, who says he was a Pharisee, not only emphasizes their belief in the resurrection as distinguishing them from the Sadducees, but also says that they stressed the traditions of the fathers. He mentions, with amazement, that the captured Pharisees still observed the food laws as they were being taken as prisoners to Rome (*Vita* 13f.) and that at the beginning of the Jewish war, he and other Pharisees were part of a delegation which collected tithes in Galilee (*Vita* 28f., 63).

This supports the evidence of the New Testament about the Pharisees. They are said to stress the 'traditions of the fathers' (Gal. 1.14; Mark 7.1ff.). They observed the Sabbath commandments (Mark 2.23–3.6 *et al.* and also in John) and the purity commandments (Mark 7.1ff.) and were strict about tithing even the most trivial agricultural products (Matt. 23.23f., Luke 18.12).

The Pharisees' criticism of Jesus, as reported in the Gospels, may reflect their closeness to him. While both wanted to hallow everyday life in the light of God's will, the Pharisees advocated a defensive notion of cleanness. Purity was to be maintained by keeping aloof from the impure, whereas Jesus advocated an offensive notion of cleanness, whereby the holy communicated that holiness to publicans and sinners.[20] Jesus seems to have made the ethical requirements of the Law more demanding while relaxing the ritual requirements.[21]

There is some suggestion that traditions in Galilee were less rigorous about purity rules. Gerd Theissen writes: 'The Pharisaic halakah (which had stricter and more liberal expressions) was hardly predominant in Galilee in the time of Jesus.'[22] He notes that Josephus says that the Zealot leader John of Gischala ate food prohibited by the Law and violated traditional rules of cleanness.[23] Galilean halakah may also have been more adapted to agricultural life, whereas the Pharisees were used to urban life. Jerusalem tended to look down on Galilee. Johann ben Zakkai (*c.* 70) is said to have exclaimed, 'Galilee, Galilee, you hate the Torah!'[24]

Those who have seen Jesus as a faithful Jew have tended to think of him as close to the Pharisees and to discount the arguments between Jesus and the Pharisees which are recorded in the Gospels as reflecting the conflict between church and synagogue in the latter half of the first century. Recent studies, however, which have shown the great religious variety and ferment in the Judaism of the first half of the century allows us now to see that there may have been disputes between Jesus and the Pharisees, but that these reflected the arguments between different Jewish groups at the time. They were internal intra-Jewish arguments. To suggest that Jesus may have been critical of some Pharisees is not to be anti-Jewish.

The Pharisees were almost certainly not involved in the plot to have Jesus put to death. Some Pharisees – Nicodemus and Joseph of Arimathea – spoke for Jesus at the Sanhedrin (John 7.45ff. and 19.38ff.). When the Sadducees took action against the early Christians (Acts 5.17), the Pharisee Gamaliel counselled caution. Later, when Paul was arrested, he also got the Pharisees on his side (Acts 23.6–7). Further, according to Josephus (*Ant.* 20.200), when the Sadducean high priest had James the brother of the Lord executed, he was then deposed because of protests from those 'loyal to the law', who were probably Pharisees. The contrast between the Sadducees and the

Pharisees, however, should not be over-emphasized. Paul, a Pharisee, is said to have set out to Damascus with the authority of the high priest to arrest any Christians there.

Scribes

It is sometimes suggested that the scribes and Pharisees were identical, but that is open to question.[25] The word 'scribe' denotes in Greek an official who could draw up a document, whether at the royal court or for a village transaction. The word had the breadth of meaning of the English word 'secretary', who can be a Secretary of State or the correspondent of a small local committee or a typist at an office. Because the Torah included legal matters, the scribe in the Jewish world was also a religious teacher and authority. The first scribe is often said to be Ezra, who was regarded as 'skilful in the Law of Moses' (Ezra 7.6). Jesus Sirach sings the praise of the scribes, whom he assumed to be from an upper class (Ecclus. 38.24ff.). Around the same time (*c.* 200 BCE) a document referred to a group of privileged scribes at the Temple in Jerusalem (Josephus, *Ant.* 12.138–144). In rabbinic writings, there are occasional references to the teaching of the scribes, but they do not seem to form a unified group.

The Gospels, however, by the way in which they set the scribes in opposition to Jesus, may give the impression that they were a unified group. Yet the contrast is primarily between the authority with which Jesus taught and the way in which the scribes referred back to scriptural texts or oral teaching. Indeed in Mark's Gospel the arguments with the scribes are mainly about authority (9.11ff.; 12.28ff.; 12.35ff.), whereas the arguments with the Pharisees are mainly about behaviour (2.13; 7.1ff.; 10.2ff.). Mark, in fact, refers specifically to the 'scribes of the Pharisees' (2.16) and mentions a scribe who was sympathetic to Jesus (12.28ff.). Matthew refers to a scribe who wanted to follow Jesus (Matt. 8.19) and seems to know of Christian scribes (13.52). Mark also seems to make a differentiation between scribes from Galilee and from Jerusalem (3.22; 7.1) and refers to the scribes or 'teachers of the law' as one of the groups who made up the Sanhedrin (10.33; 11.18; 14.1). It is noteworthy that both Jesus and

John the Baptist are addressed as 'rabbi', a title which came to be used of the scribes.

The Sadducees

The term 'Sadducee' is probably derived from 'Zadok', who was the ancestor of the high-priestly family of the Zadokites (I Chron. 24.3). They are first mentioned under John Hyrcanus (134–104 BCE), after he had broken with the Pharisees who had criticized his lack of dynastic legitimacy. It is suggested that they supported the Hasmonean policy of expansion which led to the reunion of Idumea, Samaria and Galilee with Jewish territory. As representatives of the sole legitimate high-priestly family, they would have welcomed the destruction by John Hyrcanus of the rival Samaritan temple on Mount Gerizim.

The Sadducees, unlike Jesus and the Pharisees, did not believe in the resurrection. Yet, Theissen suggests that Jesus may have borrowed some of the Sadducees' arguments to use against the Pharisees. Like the Sadducees, Jesus emphasized the present as the time of salvation and was critical of the 'traditions of the fathers'.[26]

In the first century CE they appear beside the circle of high-priestly families in the Sanhedrin. They were hostile to Jesus and his followers, partly perhaps because of Jesus' vigorous criticism of the Temple. The role of the Sadducees in bringing about the death of Jesus will be discussed in Chapter 5. Little sympathy is shown to them by either Christian or Jewish scholars, but the difficulties which Christian leaders have faced under oppressive regimes in the Soviet Union or China should make us aware of the dilemma which they faced. Is compromise which allows for survival of the cult necessarily worse than opposition which resulted in total destruction of Jerusalem? The Sadducees supported proceedings against the early Christians (Acts 5.17). Later, according to Josephus the Sadducean high priest had James the brother of the Lord executed.[27]

The Essenes

If the Sadducees compromised themselves by seeking a *modus vivendi* with the Roman authorities, the Essenes preserved their purity by withdrawing from society. The Essenes, the third group that Josephus mentions, is usually thought to be related to the Qumran community near the Dead Sea. Some recent writing has tried to link the Essenes with the Sadducees, as the 'sons of Zadok' are important in Qumran documents and because the ritual practices in the Qumran documents correspond with those espoused by the Sadducees in rabbinic literature. If there were links at one time, the two groups chose different paths. The focus of the Qumran community was study of the written word and its interpretation.

In the early first century BCE, the Essene sect numbered about four thousand. Only adult males were admitted after a three-year probationary period, when they swore an oath of secrecy about their teachings. Celibacy was enjoined. Meals were eaten in common and attention was paid to cleanliness and ritual purity. The Essenes paid careful attention to ethical behaviour. Although they were critical of the Jerusalem Temple, they sent votive offerings to it. In defence of a true obedience to God and his Torah, the Essenes were among those who fought the Romans in the first Jewish revolt.

Although the Essenes are not mentioned in the Gospels, some scholars have suggested that John the Baptist and, therefore maybe Jesus, had some links with them.

The Herodians

Another group mentioned in the Gospels were the Herodians. Herod the Great ruled Palestine as a client prince of the Romans. After his death in 4 BCE, the Roman Senate eventually confirmed his three sons in power. Half the kingdom, including Judea, was put under Archelaus, but in 6 CE the Romans removed him from power and themselves took control in Judea and Samaria. In the north Herod Antipas, who was to behead John the Baptist, ruled in Galilee and Perea and Herod Phillip was given another quarter in the northeast.

The payment of tax to the Romans was a problem of conscience for devout Jews. The Pharisees probably sympathized with the position of Judas of Galilee who held that payment to the emperor was idolatry. It was easier for Jews to pay tax to a Jewish client prince, even if he then paid tribute to the Romans. The Herodians acted in a sense as religiously neutral 'money launderers'. It is therefore quite likely that Herodians, who were supporters of the Herods, would ask Jesus about taxation (Mark 12.13). Also relevant to the Herodians was the question which, after he had cured the man with a shrivelled hand on the Sabbath, Jesus asked his critics: 'Which is lawful on the Sabbath: to do good or to do evil, to save life or to kill?' (Mark 3.6) – as the Herodians had argued that Jews had the right to fight in self-defence on the Sabbath.

Militants

If the Herodians were Roman stooges, there were others who were prepared to take up arms against the Romans. Some of them were 'Sicarii', after the Latin for dagger, *sica*. Lester Grabbe suggests they could be called 'Assassins'.[28] They concealed their daggers in their clothing, went close to an official in a crowd, and struck their victim quickly and disappeared. Josephus said that the followers of this so-called 'fourth philosophy' agreed with the Pharisees, 'except that they have a passion for liberty that is almost unconquerable, since they are convinced that God alone is their leader and master'.[29]

Although the Zealots may have had links with the Sicarii, Josephus distinguished the two groups. We know little about the origins of the Zealots, but they fought with particular bravery against the Romans during the final siege of Jerusalem. It was the Sicarii, however, who held out at Masada.[30] Luke describes one of Jesus' disciples as a Zealot (Luke 6.15), but it seems clear that Jesus rejected the use of force.

The picture that emerges of first-century Palestine is of a high degree of religious and political ferment, increased by the juxta-position of strong Hellenistic and Roman influences. There were social tensions and life was hard for the peasants and especially for those who were dispossessed from the land, but Galilee was reasonably peaceful.[31]

After the fall of Jerusalem, Judaism, under the leadership of the Rabbis, became more unified. At the time of Jesus, however, there was vigorous debate about the true way of responding to God's call.

4

JESUS AND THE JUDAISM OF
HIS DAY

So Jesus was Jewish, but that does not mean that there was no conflict between him and some religious groups. And to say that is certainly not anti-Jewish. As I write, the Labour Party in Britain is trying to select who should stand as mayor and there is no love lost between the various candidates, although they belong to the same party. In the USA, the Presidential primaries have started and rival candidates in the same party have harsh words for each other. Indeed, a newspaper headline declares 'Bad blood spilt in Democrat battle'.[1]

The Jewish groups, briefly described in the last chapter, were capable of being very rude about each other. There was also rivalry and dislike between different social and economic groups. As the American scholar Robert Funk has said, 'Scholars are in the habit of saying that Jesus was a Jew, as though that identification tells us all we need to know.'[2] It is, therefore, important where we place Jesus in the Judaism of the first century CE and this is a major concern of the most recent attempts to discover 'the historical Jesus'.

There is, however, little agreement among scholars on how this should be done. Daniel Harrington, for example, describes 'seven different images of Jesus that have been proposed by scholars in recent years, the differences relating to the different Jewish backgrounds against which they have chosen to locate their image of the historical Jesus'.[3] Jesus was pictured as a political revolutionary by S. G. F. Brandon (1967), as a magician by Morton Smith (1978), as a Galilean charismatic by Geza Vermes (1981, 1984), as a Galilean rabbi by Bruce Chilton (1984), as a Hillelite or proto-Pharisee by Harvey Falk (1985), as an Essene also by Harvey Falk (1985), and as an eschatological prophet by E. P. Sanders (1985).[4] More recent studies, such as John Dominic Crossan's view of Jesus as a peasant Jewish cynic (1992), Robert Funk's picture of him as a social rebel and iconoclast (1996), John Meier's description of him as a Marginal Jew (1991) and Gerd Theissen's portrait of Jesus as an itinerant charismatic (1998), can be added to the list.[5]

The Law

One major issue is Jesus' attitude to the Torah, which is usually, although inadequately, translated as 'Law'.[6] Some Christians write off any link between the teaching of Jesus and the Jewish Law. E. Stauffer, a German Protestant scholar, for example, said that Jesus 'is the one who announces a morality without legalism, which in principle is free of any tie to the Mosaic Torah and Jewish obedience to the Torah'.[7] Others take the opposite view. For instance, Leonard Swidler, who is Professor of Catholic Thought at Temple University, says that Jesus 'did not come to dispense with or do away with the Torah, the Law; rather he came to carry it out'.[8] Swidler refers to the Orthodox Israeli Jewish scholar, David Flusser, who said that Yeshua was 'a Torah-true Jew'.[9] Swidler also quotes Nicolas de Lange, a Jewish Professor of Rabbinics at Cambridge University, who wrote: 'Nor can I accept that Jesus' purpose was to do away with Judaism as he found it. He had his criticism, to be sure, but he wanted to perfect the law of Moses, not to annul it. The Christian hostility to this law strikes me as a betrayal of Jesus' teaching.'[10]

Jesus' attitude to the Torah is clearly an issue that Jewish and Christian scholars need to address together, without fearing that to find Jesus was critical of or even rejected the Law means a return to the Christian anti-Judaism of the past. Perhaps we can begin to see genuine value in different ways of responding to God. But before that is possible it is essential to try to understand the Judaism of the period for itself and for Christians to rid themselves of false stereotyped pictures of Judaism.

Judaism is a religion of covenant. This is made clear when a Jewish boy is circumcised. It is also evident in the Passover seder. God promised to Abraham that he would bless his descendants. God rescued the people of Israel from slavery in Egypt and chose them to be his own people. The Torah was given by God to those whom he by grace had chosen for his own. The Torah was the way of life for a community and God gave Israel the Land of Promise where it could be a holy people. Circumcision was the sign of membership of the holy people. To obey the Torah was to affirm the covenant and to accept God's promise. It was the loving response to God's gracious act of rescue and choice of Israel.

Too often Christians have pictured the Law as a burden rather than as a delight. The influence of Luther and the way Paul has often been interpreted has been strong. This attitude is reflected in hymns, like 'Rock of Ages', which has the lines

> Not the labours of my hands
> Can fulfil thy law's demands.[11]

or 'With Broken Heart', with the words

> Nor alms, nor deeds that I have done,
> Can for a single sin atone.[12]

Contrast this to Psalm 119, where the psalmist says, 'I love your commandments more than gold, more than the finest gold' (v. 127) or 'Lord how I love your law, it is my meditation all the day long' (v. 97). In fact joyful obedience, springing from thankfulness for God's mercy, is characteristic of Jewish devotion.

E. P. Sanders, in his detailed studies of Jewish material in *Paul and Palestinian Judaism* and *Jesus and Judaism*, has argued that to regard Judaism as a religion of righteousness gained by meticulous observance of the requirements of the Law 'is based on a massive perversion and misunderstanding of the material'.[13] God chose Israel. Obedience to the Torah shows a reliance on God's fidelity, not a concern to win his favour. The debates about atonement show that there was a means by which the penitent sinner could be restored to a right relationship to God, a relationship established by God's mercy and maintained by the individual's obedience and repentance and by God's forgiveness.

I think E. P Sanders is right to reject views of Judaism as a religion of 'works-righteousness'. He is probably also correct when he says that 'Jesus accepted "covenantal nomism". His mission was to Israel in the name of the God of Israel. He thus evidently accepted his people's special status, that is, the election and covenant. I think it is equally clear that he accepted obedience to the law as the norm . . .'[14] Sanders, however, to my mind, minimizes the impression given by the Gospels that Jesus often sharply disagreed with some of the Pharisees. They may, of course, reflect the understanding of the early church at the time when the Gospels took shape, but there are parallel accounts of similar sharp disagreements between leading Pharisees themselves. We know of the disputes between the followers of Hillel (late first century BCE to early first century CE) and Shammai (c. 50 BCE to c. 30 CE) and it is probable that there were at the time of Jesus more and less rigorous interpretations of the Law. Further, in the last chapter we saw that some Pharisees were very strict in their observance of the food laws and the detailed requirements of tithing. I think also that some writers underestimate the changes made by the rabbis as they re-established Judaism after the fall of Jerusalem. The Jewish scholar Pinchas Lapide, after a detailed survey, has said that 'From our contemporary vantage point we are able to affirm that the exegesis of Jesus has won out in Talmudic praxis, which at that time was still fluctuating in the process of developing into a written form. What during his lifetime was still disputed has long since become a rule of life – not least thanks to an understanding of the Torah that often is reminiscent of the exegetical manner of the Nazarene.'[15] In political and religious life, even the most traditional bodies are always changing – New Labour, for example, is not identical with Old Labour.

'Not to abolish, but to complete'

What did Jesus himself say about the Law? Matthew 5.17–20 reports Jesus as saying:

Do not suppose that I have come to abolish the Law and the prophets; I did not come to abolish, but to complete. I tell you this; so long as heaven and earth endure, not a letter, not a stroke, will disappear from the Law until all that must happen has happened. If any man therefore sets aside even the least of the Law's demands, and teaches others to do the same, he will have the lowest place in the kingdom of Heaven, whereas anyone who keeps the Law, and teaches others so, will stand high in the kingdom of heaven. I tell you, unless you show yourselves far better men than the Pharisees and the doctors of the Law, you can never enter the kingdom of Heaven (NEB).

These verses are of great importance for our views of Jesus' attitude to the Torah (Law) and therefore for our views of his relationship to the Pharisees. The New Testament scholar John Fenton says verse 18 is 'one of the most difficult verses in this Gospel'.[16]

There are many questions about this passage. First, is it authentic, or how much of it is authentic? Is the Matthean church in opposition to Hellenistic Christians, who are lax about the Law and does Matthew therefore strengthen Jesus' words? Alternatively, is it surprising that in a church engaged in strong polemic against the Pharisees, Matthew does not weaken the words of Jesus? Luke 16.17 suggests that Matthew 5.18 was already in the tradition.

Secondly, what does 'to complete' or 'to fulfil' mean? It may mean that Jesus has come to fulfil the prophecies of him in scripture. Jesus' task is not merely to affirm the Law but to actualize the will of God made known in the Bible. Fulfilment may mean going beyond the righteousness of the Pharisees, as is suggested in verse 20 and in much of the teaching in the Sermon on the Mount, although if the Sermon is not a unity but sayings collected together by the evangelist, then it is misleading to interpret this verse in the light of following verses.

Thirdly, what is signified by 'until all is accomplished'? Does it mean 'until the end of the world', which the early Christians expected to occur very soon? Does it mean 'until Jesus has fulfilled the Law' by his obedience unto death? If so, Jesus would have freed the early Christians from the Law's demands, as is perhaps suggested in Mark 7. The verse may mean 'until God's final purpose is achieved'. In that case, the Law has permanent validity.

Further when in verse 19 Jesus warns people not to set aside 'the least of the Law's demands', is he referring to the commandments of the Law or to his own teaching in the rest of the Sermon on the Mount?

How commentators interpret these verses in part reflects their answers to larger questions, such as 'Did Jesus himself obey the Law?' and 'Do the arguments with the Pharisees reflect the conflicts between church and synagogue rather than arguments between Jesus and Pharisees?'

Even if the Sermon on the Mount consists of a collection of the sayings of Jesus rather than a copy of an actual sermon, there is a consistency in his demand for a radical inner obedience to the Law's intention. It is not only murder that is wrong, anger is almost as bad. Divorce is tantamount to adultery. Love should not be restricted to neighbours but should include love for enemies. Jesus tells his disciples that there must be no limit to their goodness, just as their heavenly Father's goodness knows no bounds (Matt. 5.48). No wonder Jesus' teaching was disconcerting and amazing and that the people commented on the authority with which he spoke (Mark 1.22).

Jesus largely formulated his ethic in wisdom-type admonitions and sentences. In speaking both of marriage and the Sabbath, he referred back to God's purpose in creation (Mark 10.2–9; 2.27). In Matthew 5.43, the sun is the model for love of the enemy. The freedom of his attitude to Torah may reflect that of the wisdom tradition, as wisdom teaching made little direct reference to the Torah. The Wisdom of Jesus Sirach (the book of Ecclesiasticus), for example, nowhere directly quotes and expounds the Torah, although the book is a testimony to upright Torah piety and Jesus Sirach identifies Wisdom with the Torah (Sir. 24.23).

Jesus illustrated his teaching by using parables. He was not alone in this. Parables are increasingly recognized to have been a popular form of oral religious instruction at the time of Jesus. His parables have a very polished narrative structure, often with more than one scene, different groups of workers and a dialogue. There is also a distinctive balancing of God's justice and generosity, which includes the marginalized.[17]

The parables of the Prodigal Son (Luke 15.11–32) or the Labourers in the Vineyard (Matt. 20.1–16) suggest that Jesus, like many mystics, had a sense of the boundless goodness of God. If so, it is not surprising that he was impatient with the restrictive regulations that often characterize religious communities. It was agreed that saving life overrode Sabbath restrictions on work. But if a man had been blind from birth or had a withered arm, could his healing not wait for one more day (John 9; Mark 3.4)? No, not if you put yourself in the blind man's shoes; but, yes if you were preoccupied with religious rules.

Did it really matter, if the disciples were hungry and plucked some ears of grain on the Sabbath? It reminds me of the discussions when I was first ordained about the practice of fasting or not eating before receiving communion. If you felt you might faint, would it be a great sin to have a cup of tea before setting out for the early service? Indeed, one objection to evening communion services was that people could not be expected to fast until the evening. These were real discussions thirty years ago, which is a reminder how quickly accepted religious practice can change.

With regards to the Sabbath commandment, Jesus gave priority to healing, even if the illness was not life-threatening and it may be that his itinerant lifestyle made it impossible to keep all the usual requirements.

His impatience was shown in his healing ministry. In his work as a healer and exorcist, Jesus has been compared to various miracle workers of that time: to the Hellenistic or the magician,[18] to the rabbinic charismatic miracle-worker,[19] and to Jewish sign prophets.[20] The uniqueness of Jesus' approach, which has been seen both in eschatological terms by Gerd Theissen,[21] who sees them as demonstrating in the present the future universal salvation, and as a subversive social challenge by John Dominic Crossan,[22] lies in the fact 'that the healings and exorcisms which take place in the present are accorded an eschatological significance' – a sign of a new world order.

In his compassion, Jesus is shown to ignore society's usual divisions. He was prepared to touch and heal a man with leprosy, although such people were regarded then, as in many societies, as unclean and kept at a distance (Mark 1.40ff.). He was prepared to eat with tax collectors and publicans (Mark 2.16). In answer to the lawyer's question, 'Who is my neighbour?', Jesus told a story about a man who fell among thieves and was helped by a Samaritan – the religious people in the story may have been afraid of being defiled by touching a dead body – and then asked 'who behaved as a neighbour to the man who had been attacked?' (Luke 10.25 ff.). He did not object to the woman with an issue of blood touching him (Mark 5.25 ff.). He overcame his own hesitations and healed the daughter of the Syro-Phoenician woman (Mark 7.24 ff.). He defied custom in accepting a drink from a Samaritan woman (John 4.7).

Indeed several passages in the Gospels show Jesus' open and respectful attitude to women, but as Theissen warns, a false contrast with the Judaism of his day should be avoided.

> A pattern of explanation widespread in scholarship, according to which Jesus with his friendly attitudes towards women was an exception among his patriarchal Jewish contemporaries, and women, if they accepted his message, were at the same time liberated from a Jewish law which despised women, is more nourished by triumphalist and anti-Jewish motives than supported by the sources. Rather, we must note that the Jesus movement was a movement within Judaism. The tension recognizable in the attitude towards women between unbroken patriarchal and emancipatory tendencies reflects a process of discussion within Palestinian society which increased under Hellenistic influence. Moreover, a warning should be issued against the over-hasty assumption that women always or indeed exclusively heard and judged Jesus' message in relation to their gender.[23]

Not all the details of the stories about Jesus may be accurate. Even of a near contemporary such as Princess Diana, many stories are told. Some may be apocryphal and yet they illustrate the impression she

made on people who met her. The stories of Jesus also have a cumulative effect. They suggest someone who was not challenging the
Law, *per se,* but was critical of restrictive interpretations which
seemed to make rules more important than people. 'The Sabbath',
he said, 'was made for man, not man for the Sabbath' (Mark 2.27).
Jesus criticized those who avoided their responsibilities to their
parents by dedicating their possessions to God (Mark 7.9 ff.). He
warned the Pharisees that they had neglected the more important
matters of the Law, 'justice, mercy and faithfulness' (Matt. 23.23)

Eschatology

To what extent was Jesus' teaching shaped by his expectation of an
imminent end to the world? This has been a matter of prolonged
debate, and eschatology has hovered over twentieth-century New
Testament studies just as the nuclear threat has overshadowed
society.

There was great variety of eschatological expectation in first-
century Judaism. There were those who believed that in a new age,
there would be a new temple and that both the outcasts of Israel
would be gathered in and even the Gentiles. If, as is possible, Jesus
believed that with his ministry a new age was dawning, then his over-
turning of tables in the Temple and his welcome for outcasts would
fit with this belief.[24] Marcus Borg, however, with other recent North
American writers, has challenged the emphasis on eschatology that
has dominated New Testament studies.[25] Borg, according to a
quotation from Richard A. Horsley, another leading North
American New Testament scholar, on the cover of his book,
'presents an understandable figure with whom most North
American Christians will be comfortable'. A rather questionable
recommendation, as most portraits of Jesus present him as a figure
disturbing both to his contemporaries and to subsequent generations.

Borg is right to redress the balance and he argues a well-nuanced
case. Theissen, however, holds that Jesus' teaching about the kingdom corresponds to the main tradition of Judaism, arguing that 'the

kingly rule of God which stands at the centre of the preaching of Jesus can only be understood in terms of the centre of Jewish belief in God. Jesus is not "a marginal Jew" in his eschatological preaching. Rather, in it he responds to the basic problem of Jewish monotheism.'[26]

It seems that to underline the immediacy of his warnings, Jesus drew on eschatological themes of apocalyptic writers. His ethical teaching was set in the context of his message about the coming kingdom, which gave urgency both to his call for repentance and assurance to his promise of salvation for the poor. Compared to the apocalyptic writings of the time, Jesus avoided cosmological speculation.

Indeed, from both the wisdom and apocalyptic traditions, Jesus took over only what is ethically relevant. Compared to the teachings of the Qumran community, where obedience to the Torah was grounded in scripture as understood on the basis of its authoritative interpretation by the Teacher of Righteousness, Jesus could play off one passage of scripture against another (Mark 10.11 ff.).

It seems, therefore, that as K. Berger says, Jesus drew on various strands of contemporary Judaism 'which stressed the primacy of the ethical, whilst allowing some relaxation of the ritual requirements'.[27]

Jesus, therefore, both affirmed the eternity of the Torah (Matt. 5.18) but also its temporal limitation (Matt. 11.12). As Gerd Theissen puts it:

> We can establish that the ethical preaching of Jesus corresponds precisely to the three sources of Jewish ethics: the Torah at the centre, with wisdom and eschatology alongside it. At its centre it is orientated on the Torah; however, it is orientated on a Torah read in the prophetic spirit. No scribe, but a charismatic, has interpreted the Torah here. From this centre Jesus appropriates ideas from wisdom and apocalyptic. That becomes particularly clear if we look at the centre of his ethic: the command to love.[28]

It is clear that Jesus' actions and the disputes they engendered are not an attack on Judaism. They raise questions which are still vital on the balance between the boundless mercy of God and the demands of discipleship. At one of my churches for a time, we were joined by a self-proclaimed 'gay messiah' who, with his hat on, sat in the front pew. Most of the congregation were willing to tolerate his idiosyncrasies, but some felt we were irreverent and indeed even condoning immoral behaviour. One way to be holy is to withdraw, 'to keep oneself unspotted by the world' (James 1.27) and to set up barriers that keep the rest of society at a distance. This is even more the case in societies where great importance is attached to purity.

Marcus Borg[29] gives particular attention to the question of purity. A 'purity' society, he says, is explicitly organized around the polarities of pure and impure, clean and unclean. It applies not only to behaviour, but to people and social classes. An example is the traditional Brahmin (Hindu) society. As a student in India I had invitations to visit a number of Brahmin families. I was at that time a carnivore and this created problems for some of my hosts. One person was happy to entertain me at a restaurant, but explained he could not invite me to his home because his mother would feel my presence defiled her home and kitchen. A concern for purity underlies some of the caste rules about whom you could eat with or indeed even touch.

Borg argues that first-century Jewish Palestine was a purity society. Its core value was crystallized in the verse 'You shall be holy as God is holy' (Lev. 19.2). He points out that the gradations of the purity system correlated with the descending ladder of a peasant society and that the purity system was the ideology of the ruling elite. Jesus' apparent disregard for purity requirements was, therefore, a much more serious matter than many Western commentators would recognize. Traditional Indian society was scandalized by Gandhi opening the temples to the Harijans or outcastes, just as white supremacists in the USA were threatened by Martin Luther King. The apartheid regime in South Africa also used colour and racial barriers to prolong its political and economic power. Jesus' willingness to touch and heal those with leprosy, to take water from a Samaritan woman or to eat with unwashed hands in the company of publicans and sinners, was not only defiance of accepted norms of behaviour but a subversive challenge to the economic and power structures of the society. Indeed, Borg says that the 'act of over-turning "money tables" in the temple is most plausibly seen as a protest against the temple as the centre of an exploitative social-economic system'.[30] Further, Jesus' teaching has been described as subversive wisdom – challenging the accepted norms of society. John Dominic Crossan sums up his brilliant book, *The Historical Jesus*, by saying that 'The historical Jesus was a peasant Jewish cynic. . . His strategy, implicitly for himself and explicitly for his followers, was the combination of free healing and common eating, a religious and economic egalitarianism that negated alike and at once the hier-archical and paternal normalcies of Jewish religion and Roman power.'[31]

If like me your sympathy is with those who emphasize the ethical rather than purity concerns and ritual, it needs to be recognized how easily religious values are corroded by the surrounding society. This would be the complaint made against many liberal Christians today. In the centuries before Jesus Jews had had to struggle, even at the cost of martyrdom, against the all-pervasive Hellenism which was eroding Jewish values and practice. Some Jews, for example, who wished to take part in games and wrestling wanted their circum-cision – the sign of the covenant – disguised.

It is also not self-evident that an inclusive fellowship is better than an exclusive one. Looking back, one would have wished that more German Christians in the 1930s, like members of the Confessing Church, had vigorously opposed the Nazis. Under Communist regimes, there were Christians who tried to establish a *modus vivendi* with the government to preserve the church and others who risked their lives in challenging the state. Again, was the church which reached agreement with the Roman emperors more faithful than the Jewish people who upheld the Torah through centuries of persecution?

Crossan puts this very clearly:

By the end of the first century two great religions, rabbinic Judaism and early Christianity, were emerging from a common matrix. Each claimed to be its only legitimate continuation and each had texts and traditions to prove that claim. Each, in fact, represented an equally valid, equally surprising, and equally magnificent leap out of the past and into the future. It would, in truth, be difficult to say, had Moses awoke from slumber around 200 CE, which of the two would have surprised him more. I insist once more that in linking exclusive Judaism with rabbinic Judaism and inclusive Judaism with Christianity, I am not making a comparison pejorative in either direction. To be human is to balance particularity and universality, and, although the balance may always tip one way or the other, either extreme is equally inhuman. You can lose your soul at either end of the spectrum, and one can and should ask, with equal legitimacy: did Judaism give too little in failing to convert the Roman Empire? Did Christianity give too much in succeeding?[32]

The point is that the conflicts between Jesus and various of his contemporaries are complex and that similar issues recur. There is no need to pretend disagreements did not take place, but equally Jewish and Christian scholars should, at last, be able to highlight the issues without the long shadow of anti-Semitism. Besides, Jesus' radical call to mirror the compassion of God, which know no limits, is as much a challenge to Christians today as it was to many of his Jewish contemporaries.

5

THE DEATH OF JESUS

The most dangerous aspect of Christian anti-Jewish polemic has been the teaching of 'deicide'. For centuries the church claimed that although Jesus was the Messiah foretold in the Old Testament, the Jews not only failed to recognize him, but were also responsible for his death ('deicide'). Although this teaching has now been repudiated by almost all churches, any reading of the Gospels' account of Jesus' passion is liable to reawaken this ancient prejudice. This was brought home to me when I was asked to comment on a draft of a new popular life of Jesus. I complained that it was anti-Jewish and the author said, 'I have only been summarizing the New Testament.'

In recent years, it has been fashionable among scholars, rightly in my view, to put the blame for the death of Jesus on the Romans, but anti-Semitism is too pernicious to be left to the vagaries of scholarly fashion. So, although I shall first look at historical reconstructions of what happened, I shall also ask how the liturgical use of the Gospel account of Jesus' death can avoid covert anti-Judaism.

Deicide

Martin Gilbert begins his thorough account of the Holocaust with these words: 'For many centuries, primitive Christian Europe had regarded the Jew as the "Christ-killer": an enemy and a threat to be converted and so be "saved", or to be killed'.[1] Lord Runcie, former Archbishop of Canterbury, recognized this at a Kristallnacht Memorial meeting in 1988, when he said: 'For centuries Christians have held Jews collectively responsible for the death of Jesus. On

Good Friday Jews have, in times past, cowered behind locked doors for fear of a Christian mob seeking "revenge" for deicide. Without the poisoning of Christian minds through centuries, the Holocaust is unthinkable.'[2]

In fairness to the churches, it should be said that this teaching was never used to justify mass murder. Jews in Christendom had a protected if abject position and at times church authorities protected them against the indebted barons and the people. The purpose of the teaching about deicide was used to explain why the Jews were a reprobate people, rejected and punished by God. Inevitably it fed popular prejudice and, even more tragically, it was to hand when Hitler wanted to use it for his evil purposes – even though he was anti-Christian as well as anti-Jewish.[3] Even today, as year by year millions of Christians listen to the story of Jesus' passion, it is important to make clear why the Gospel narratives should not be taken at face value.

Historical reliability

Inevitably, a major issue is the reliability of the Gospels. This question is highlighted by the dispute between Raymond Brown, who died recently, whose monumental two-volume study *The Death of the Messiah* was published in the early 1990s and John Dominic Crossan, whose *Who Killed Jesus?* was published in 1996.

Crossan summed up the dispute in these words: 'Basically the issue is whether the passion accounts are prophecy historicized or history remembered. Ray Brown is 80 percent in the direction of history remembered. I'm 80 percent in the opposite direction.'[4] The point is whether stories of, for example, the mocking describe an actual event to which texts from the Hebrew Bible were attached or whether those texts created the story which was then given a historical format. A further difference is that Crossan gives weight to the account of the passion recorded in the apocryphal Gospel of Peter. He and some other scholars hold that this account, in which almost every sentence is composed from references or allusions to the psalms or prophets, was the first to be written. There is not room to discuss this issue in full. In brief, the less historical basis one sees to the stories of the mocking and abuse of Jesus by the Jews, the less grounds there are for regarding the Jews as the enemies of Jesus. This imposes a grave responsibility on all who preach or teach the passion story not to reinforce the false stereotypes of the Jewish people that have bedevilled the last two thousand years.

My own position is similar to that of Simon Légasse in his *The Trial of Jesus*. He writes that it would be a mistake to relegate the 'Gospel accounts of the passion to the realm of pious legend with no historical substance. In reality these accounts embroider a basic tradition; this tradition has certainly been rearranged, but its origin is to be put in the circle of the first witnesses to the events. So the use of the Gospels is imperative . . . making use of a healthy literary and historical criticism.'[5]

Blaming the Jews

Christians who suffered persecution from the Romans would have wished to downplay the royal claims of their Master. They also tried to suggest that Pilate, the Roman governor, considered Jesus to be innocent and was pressurized into condemning him to death by the Jewish leaders. The Gospels, therefore, pin the blame for Jesus' crucifixion on the Jewish leaders.

The question of responsibility is most clearly raised by Matthew. The initiative to kill Jesus was taken by the chief priests and elders (Matt. 26.2–3). Judas, one of the disciples, then offered to betray Jesus (Matt. 26.14–16), but he later admitted that he had betrayed an innocent man and flung back at the chief priests the reward that they had given him (Matt. 27.3–10). Then after Jesus had been handed over to the Romans by the chief priests, first Pilate's wife warned her husband to 'have nothing to do with that innocent man' (Matt. 27.19), then Pilate himself washed his hands 'in full view of the people', saying, 'My hands are clean of this man's blood: see to that yourselves', to which the people 'with one voice' replied in those fateful words, 'His blood be on us, and on our children' (Matt. 27.24–26).

The other Gospels also exonerate the Romans from responsibility. In Luke's Gospel, Pilate explicitly declared that he and Herod had found no guilt in Jesus (23.13–5). In John's Gospel, Jesus said, 'he who delivered me to you has the greater sin' (19.11). The reference is almost certainly to the high priest, although it could be to Judas.

Thus, in wanting to exonerate Pilate and the Romans, the evangelists had to find another scapegoat on whom to pin responsibility for the death of Jesus – and they fixed the blame on the high priest and Jewish leaders who are said to have stirred up the opposition of the people. But is this what actually happened?

It seems very unlikely that Pilate would have executed Jesus just to please the Jewish rulers. Other evidence suggests that Pilate viewed them with contempt. Philo speaks of Pilate's 'ceaseless and supremely grievous cruelty'.[6] Anyone who was said to claim to be a king was likely to be in trouble with the Romans. It is probable that by the time the Gospels were written, Christians wanted to gain legitimacy in Roman eyes and shifted the blame for Jesus' death on to the Jews.

But can the Jewish leaders be completely exonerated from all responsibility? Severe doubts have been cast on the accuracy of the Jewish trials. They appear to break most of the rules of procedure, but would one expect the evangelists to be familiar with the legal details? I write as impeachment proceedings are starting against President Clinton, but I doubt whether all the political commentators are aware of all the legal procedures. Paul Winter[7] tried to clear the Jewish leaders of all involvement in the death of Jesus by arguing that the Sanhedrin did have the power to execute those whom it condemned. As it was the Romans, not the Jews, who put Jesus to death, Winter argues, it was clearly the Romans who took the initiative to kill him. It is, however, unlikely that the Jews had the right to put anyone to death.

Executed by the Romans

Although the Gospels agree that Jesus suffered crucifixion, which was a Roman penalty, they give the impression that the real responsibility for Jesus' death lay with the Jewish leaders and the crowd.

John when he reports the Jewish leaders as saying, 'We are not allowed to execute anyone' (18.31) was probably correct. Analogies from other provinces show that the Romans did not let capital sentences out of their hands. Josephus makes clear that Coponius (6–9 CE), the first prefect over Judea, was given all powers including the *ius gladii* (BJ 2, 117). According to Talmudic tradition the right to hold trials on capital charges was withdrawn from the Jews 'forty years' before the destruction of the Temple in 70 CE. 'Forty years' is a round number and the reference may be to the beginning of direct Roman rule in 6 CE.[8]

Admittedly, Stephen was stoned (Acts 7.54–60). Some scholars suggest that the Temple law which warned any Gentile who penetrated the inner Temple precinct that he would 'have only himself to blame that his death ensues'[9] may have been extended to cover other offences. It may, however, be that the Council took the law into their own hands. That was what happened when James the brother of the Lord was condemned to death by the Sanhedrin in 62 CE. James was killed during a vacancy following the death of the procurator Festus and before the accession to office of his successor Albinus. The high priest responsible, Ananus, was subsequently removed from office because he had exceeded his powers.[10]

Pilate, as the Roman ruler, gave the order for Jesus' crucifixion, but was it Pilate's decision? Pilate's action against Jesus could have been a *coercitio* or a *cognitio*. The first, a *coercitio*, allowed a Roman governor to use all necessary means to maintain public order – this in effect sanctioned arbitrary arrest and execution. A *cognitio*, by contrast, was a formal procedure according to rules of law. It would consist of an accusation, interrogation, perhaps a confession of guilt and the verdict.[11] Silence was regarded as a confession of guilt (John 19.10). The notice on the cross, the *titulus* that Jesus was 'the King of the Jews', suggests there was a formal charge. Jesus may have been charged with *lasae maiestatis*, which amounted to bringing Roman rule into disrespect. Tacitus noted that trials on a charge of *lasae maiestatis* were on the increase at that time (*Annals* 2.50 and 3.38).

If the charge that Jesus was 'the King of the Jews' was serious and not ironic, Jesus was condemned as a rebel. In John's Gospel there are references to his followers calling Jesus a 'king' (1.49; 6.15; 12.13) and, according to Luke, the Palm Sunday crowd shouted out, 'Blessings on him who comes as king in the name of the Lord' (19.38 NEB; cf. Luke 19.11). Jesus' death would have been a warning to other potential rebels, although he was not perhaps considered very dangerous, as the Romans appear to have made no attempt to round up his followers.

Were the Jewish leaders involved?

If the main responsibility for the execution of Jesus rests with Pilate, did some of the Jewish leaders collude with Pilate? Was Jesus, besides being a political menace, also a threat to the priestly establishment?

All the Gospels, despite significant disagreements, indicate that the chief priests and elders seized Jesus, tried him and handed him over to Romans. The Gospel narratives suggest three reasons why the Jewish authorities condemned Jesus.

One was his criticism of the Temple, which all the Gospels mention.[12] When Jesus overturned the tables and drove out the money-changers, this was probably not just an attempt to purify it of corruption, but an attack on the sacrificial system or at least a warning that it was to disappear with the coming of a new age.[13] It was certainly dangerous to attack the Temple. Centuries before, when Jeremiah prophesied that the first Temple would be destroyed, the 'prophets, priests and all the people seized him and said, "You must die"' (Jer. 26.8). According to Josephus[14] Samaritans who defended the legitimacy of their Temple were executed. The Qumran 'Teacher of Righteousness' was persecuted, among other things, because of his criticism of the Temple and the 'Wicked Priest' even attempted to kill him on the Day of Atonement. Jesus the son of Ananias was accused because of his prophecy against the Temple and the city, but was released by the Roman procurator.

The second charge against Jesus was of false prophecy and leading the people astray, which according to Deuteronomy was deserving of death (Deut. 13 and 17). Mishnaic law distinguishes between a *mesith* who leads an individual astray into idolatry and a *maddiach*, who leads the whole people astray. In the case of those so accused, the usual rules for a trial could be put aside. One might proceed with guile and kill the person concerned at the time of a festival.

One Jewish source, indeed, says that Jesus was executed as a *mesith*:

> On the Sabbath of the Passover festival Jesus (Yeshu) the Nazarene was hanged. For forty days before the execution took place, a herald went forth and cried: 'Here is Jesus the Nazarene, who is going forth to be stoned because he has practised sorcery and enticed Israel to apostasy. Anyone who can say anything in his favour, let him come forth and plead on his behalf.' But since nothing was brought forth in his favour, he was hanged on the eve of the Passover . . .[15]

Certainly this passage is unhistorical in assuming that the whole process was carried out by the Jewish authorities alone, but Christian sources mention the accusation that Jesus led the people astray (Matt. 27.63; John 7.12).[16]

The third charge against Jesus was that he claimed to be the Messiah (Mark 14.61–62). There is, however, no other evidence that the claim to be a Messiah was a criminal offence or regarded as blasphemy. Simon Bar Kochba, for example, was recognized by Rabbi Akiba as Messiah. If Jesus claimed to be divine, then that might be considered blasphemous. In Matthew, Jesus does not give a direct reply to the high priest's demand, 'I adjure you by the living God, tell us if you are the Christ, the Son of God' (Matt. 26.63). Even in Mark, both high priest and Jesus avoid directly pronouncing the name of God. Mark's use of the term 'Son of God' at key moments in his Gospel suggests that this is his own way of explaining the significance of Jesus. To Mark, the key issue between those who believed in Jesus and those who did not was whether they regarded Jesus as Messiah and Son of God. In my view, Mark's account of the trial before the high priest is a theological statement rather than an accurate historical report.

Even so, the fact that some of Jesus' followers may have spoken of him as the Messiah – even if he did not claim the title for himself – may have been politically alarming for the high priest and his advisers. They were well aware that the Romans were on the lookout to deprive them of what very limited autonomy they still possessed. Pilate might well have been glad of an excuse to curb the privileges of the Temple. To the high priests, Jesus was a political danger. 'If we let him go on like this,' John reports them as saying, 'then the Romans will come and take away both our place (or Temple) and our nation' (John 11.48). This is, of course, what happened later in the century when there was an uprising against the Roman authorities, although John may ironically imply that had the Jewish leaders listened to Jesus and his way of peace such a tragedy could have been avoided.

The Jewish leaders may then have had reason to collude with the Romans to get Jesus out of the way, although it seems clear that the Pharisees were not involved in this plot.[17]

Jewish trials of Jesus

The next question is whether the Jewish authorities followed due legal processes and indeed whether the Gospel accounts of the Jewish trials of Jesus have any basis in history. There are those, like J. Blinzler,[18] who regard them as historical and others, like H. Lietzmann,[19] who regard them as unhistorical and invented to 'exonerate the Romans'.

One problem is that the trials as reported in the Gospels do not follow the procedures laid down in the Mishnah.[20] Yet it may be that these represent Pharisaic law which was not as harsh as the Sadducean law by which Jesus would have been tried.

According to the Mishnah:

(1) capital trials may only take place in daylight, whereas, except for Luke 22.66 f., the proceedings against Jesus are at night;

(2) court proceedings may not take place on the Sabbath, on festivals and the corresponding day of rest, whereas according to the Synoptics, Jesus' trial takes place in Passover night and according to John in the night of the day of rest;

(3) a death sentence may not be passed on the first day of the trial, but only in a new session on the following day. Jesus seems to have been condemned at the first session, although Mark 15.1 records a second trial, saying, 'Very early in the morning, the chief priests, with the elders, the teachers of the law and the whole Sanhedrin reached a decision. They bound Jesus, led him away and turned him over to Pilate';

(4) According to Sanh VII, 5, blasphemy consists in speaking the name of God, but as we have seen both the high priest and Jesus avoided doing this;

(5) the regular place of assembly is the hall of cut stone in the Temple, whereas according to the Gospels, the session of the Sanhedrin took place in the palace of the high priest.[21]

J. Gnilka and others think that the interrogation of Jesus by the high priests and some members of the Sanhedrin which prepared a charge to be presented to Pilate may have been historical. R. E. Brown argues that a formal session of the Sanhedrin resolved on Jesus' death some time before his arrest (John 11.47 ff., Mark 11.18 and 14. 1–2) and that after his arrest, there was an interrogation. Brown suggests that Mark fused several processes into a kerygmatically impressive narrative.[22] He concludes:

In my judgment, two observations may be made. First, most likely, the theory of two major assemblies in the Jerusalem of Jesus' time is a wrong interpretation of the evidence whether in Josephus or the NT. With even greater surety, nothing in Jewish or Christian memory of the treatment of Jesus encourages us to believe that more than one Jewish assembly dealt with him – an assembly of the type that the Romans dealt with in negotiating with the Jews. Second, the Mishna must be understood as anachronistic in attempting to read back the Beth-Din of scholars into this earlier period.[23]

Légasse suggests that after Jesus was arrested he was taken to the house of Annas, where he was held overnight. Probably, there was an informal hearing, for, although Caiaphas was the high priest, his father-in-law Annas continued to exert his influence over the whole hierarchy. In the morning, the high priests may have involved some other members of the Sanhedrin in a further examination of Jesus so that they could prepare the charges against him that they were to present to Pilate.[24]

In my view, the Gospels do not give an accurate account of the legal proceedings, but they may recall some form of legal enquiry or interrogation conducted by the high priests, who on this occasion, perhaps because of Jesus' attacks on the Temple, of which they were the guardians, were glad to show Pilate that they were in control.

Were the Jewish people involved?

If the high priests may have been involved in the death of Jesus, the Gospels, despite Matthew's fateful words, 'His blood be on us and on our children' (27.25) suggest that he was popular with many of the people. Jesus had to be arrested in secret for fear of the people (Mark 14.1–2). In Luke, the crowd called for his execution, but a large number of people, including many women, lamented for him. Just as one thief reviled him and the other called for his help, so Luke suggests that there was a division of opinion among the people. It is noteworthy that in John it is the chief priests and their officials who shouted 'Crucify, Crucify', whereas in Mark they stir up the people to do so. Yet it is John who uses the blanket word 'Jews' of the opponents of Jesus. It is likely that some of the people were sympathetic to Jesus and that some joined their leaders in condemning him. There may have been a difference between those who followed him from Galilee and some inhabitants of Jerusalem who depended on the Temple for their livelihood. Despite popular Christian devotion, there is no reason to identify the crowd who welcomed Jesus on Palm Sunday with the crowd who called for his death.

I agree with John Dominic Crossan that the words 'His blood be on us and on our children' are Matthew's own, although Raymond

Brown, while seeing them as a Matthean composition, thinks they were based on a popular tradition and that 'there may have been a small historical nucleus, but the detection of that nucleus is beyond our grasp'.[25] One suggestion is that in these words Matthew voices his frustration with the Jewish leadership and others who brought the destruction of Jerusalem by the Romans on themselves by their refusal to follow the way of Jesus. Josephus makes clear that the fall of Jerusalem and the destruction of the Temple in 70 CE caused much self-examination among God's people as to what they had done that could have caused God to punish them thus. Matthew, writing after 70, vocalizes a causal judgment that arose among Jewish believers in Jesus, namely, that the decisive factor contributing to the catastrophe was the giving over of the innocent Son of God to crucifixion by the Romans.[26]

How to interpret Matthew 27.25

Whatever the historical origins of the words 'His blood be on us and on our children', these words, read every passiontide in churches throughout Christendom and repeated in countless passion plays, have been a cause of immense suffering to the Jewish people and have been repudiated by the churches. It is important that during passiontide those who lead worship make clear that, even if some Jews were involved in a plot to kill Jesus, the blame for his death must not be placed on all Jews at that time and certainly not on Jews of succeeding generations. It would in any case be morally wrong to hold a whole people for ever guilty for a miscarriage of justice. The British have to apologize enough for their imperial record without that burden!

Theologically, as the Vatican Council and other church synods have affirmed, God's covenant with the Jewish people has never been broken. According to Christian teaching, the death of Jesus was willed by God. Peter, in the Acts of the Apostles, recognized that the Jewish leaders acted in ignorance and that God fulfilled the prophecies by allowing his Messiah to be put to death and raised on the third day (Acts 3.17–18). Traditionally the churches have taught that Christ died for all people. All humanity, not one special group, bears collective guilt for the death of Christ. 'When the death of Jesus is seen as reason to castigate (and even to kill) Jews, the point of Jesus' death has been completely subverted.'[27]

It is perhaps helpful to refocus the question, as Ellis Rivkin has suggested. Instead of asking *who* killed Jesus, it is better to ask *what* killed Jesus. 'What emerges with great clarity,' Rivkin says, 'both from Josephus and from the Gospels, [is] that the culprit is not the Jews but the Roman imperial system', which sucked even a few Jews into its service and crucified thousands of Jews, including Jesus, in the first century.[28] That imperial system is still evident in the economic and political forces which dominate our world and allow millions to live and die in poverty and callously tolerates torture and the needless cruel and violent death of many people.

It is vital, in my view, that readings of the passion are properly introduced and put in context. It may often be better to use the phrase 'the enemies of Jesus' rather than 'the Jews'. Above all, the drama of the crucifixion should be shown to highlight the complexity, the compromise and cruelty of the human heart and to point to the way of non-violence and forgiveness which can set us free from the legacy of bitterness and hatred.

6

THE RESURRECTION

By making the resurrection an objective event in history rather than an affirmation of faith in the way of Christ, Christians have used the resurrection as a weapon with which to argue that Christianity is right and blessed by God, whereas Judaism is wrong and condemned by God. Emphasis on the resurrection has also diverted attention from the continuing evil and injustice of the world and diverted attention to the next life.

'Alleluia, Christ is risen: he is risen indeed!' Although Jews and Christians may celebrate Passover and Easter at the same time, it is this Christian affirmation that separates the two communities. The defining belief of the Christian church is that God raised Jesus from the dead.

In the past, it has been the death of Jesus, for which Jews have been blamed, that has been the cause of the greatest bitterness between the two communities, but as a measure of unanimity is reached about the events leading up to the death of Jesus, the resurrection becomes the focus of disagreement. This is particularly so if the resurrection is seen as a vindication of Jesus over against his Jewish opponents. Such a view is often linked to thinking that Jesus was critical of the Judaism of his time, but, as I have suggested, Jesus should be seen as a faithful Jew. If that is the case, the resurrection should not be preached as if it were God's way of saying that Jesus was right and Judaism was wrong. Even so, it is by the resurrection that Jesus is affirmed as Lord and Christ (Acts 2.36). Is it possible to make that affirmation without implicit criticism of Judaism? Is it possible to confess that Jesus was raised from the dead in a way that does not imply that the religious vitality of Judaism was at an end? Is it also possible for Jews, without themselves making that affirmation, to see the Christian confession as a legitimate response to the One God?

Discussion of the resurrection involves a number of complex questions. There is first the historical question of what happened. Second, what meaning did the early Christians put upon the resurrection? Third, should Christians today give the same meaning to the resurrection?

The third question is particularly acute in the shadow of both the Shoah in which six million Jews were murdered and of the other acts of genocide which have stained the twentieth century. Easter sermons which declare the victory of life over death, of good over evil and of love over hatred have a hollow ring.

There are Christians who have said that after the Holocaust, Christians should no longer proclaim the resurrection. Alice and Roy Eckardt, for example, in a famous passage at the end of their *Long Night's Journey Into Day*, wrote:

> That young Jewish prophet from Galilee sleeps now. He sleeps with the other Jewish dead, with all the disconsolate and scattered ones of the murder camps and with the unnumbered dead of the human and non-human family. But Jesus of Nazareth shall be raised. So too shall the small Hungarian children of Auschwitz. Once upon a time, they shall again play and they shall again laugh. The little one of Terezin shall see another butterfly. We shall all sing, and we shall all dance. And we shall love one another.[1]

Others such as the Roman Catholic scholar John Pawlikowski, for example, make the incarnation central as 'the manifestation of the divine-human nexus'. 'Put somewhat simply,' he writes, 'what ultimately came to be recognized with clarity for the first time through the ministry and person of Jesus was how profoundly integral humanity was to the self-definition of God. This in turn implied that each human person is somehow divine, that he or she somehow shares in the constitutive nature of God. Christ is the theological symbol that the church selected to try to express this reality.'[2]

What happened?

The coming into existence of a community that believed that Jesus had been raised from the dead by God is historically certain. This is the distinctive belief to be found in most of the books of the New Testament.

What actually happened is historically uncertain. This is true of all the Gospel records of Jesus' life and ministry, but there are particular difficulties attached to the accounts of his resurrection. For example, was Mark's Gospel intended to end at verse eight of chapter sixteen or is the final section of the Gospel missing? Is the last chapter of St John's Gospel an appendix that was added later? Were the appearances of the Risen Christ all in the Jerusalem area, as Luke suggests, or were some also in Galilee?

The witness of the early Christians is based on the scriptures, on the appearances and on the empty tomb.

The early Christians argued that the suffering and resurrection of the Messiah was foretold in the Hebrew Bible (Acts 2.24–25; Luke 24.26; Rom. 15.3). To the disciples walking to Emmaus, the 'stranger' explained, 'Was not the Messiah bound to suffer thus before entering upon his glory?' The early Christians spoke of the resurrection as a new Exodus (Luke 9.30; I Cor. 10.4; I Peter 1.18) and as a new birth (I Peter 1.3). It is not clear how far this interpretation reflected the teaching of Jesus himself. It certainly implied reading the Hebrew Bible with new presuppositions. The argument from scripture is an interpretation of what was claimed to have happened, but not evidence in itself for the resurrection.

The main evidence is the witness of the disciples that the Risen Christ had appeared to them. The first witnesses were women who came early to the tomb. The evidence of women was not accepted in Jewish courts at that time. All of those who are recorded as having seen the Risen Lord were members of the believing community. The appearances were not public events.

How do we picture the Risen Christ? Did the disciples see a re-animated corpse? No: the Risen One could pass through doors. Did the disciples have a spiritual vision? Perhaps, but the Risen Lord asked for food and invited Thomas to touch him. Paul' s phrase 'a spiritual body' is helpful. The disciples would have been aware of the Pharisaic belief in the resurrection so the idea was not strange to them.[3] It may be that psychic studies and our knowledge of telepathy and depth psychology are helpful. I do not think we can be clear about what happened. There is an element of reserve and mystery about the accounts of the appearances of the Risen Lord which is appropriate to any attempt to communicate a profound spiritual experience.

Even the empty tomb is not a public event. It has been said that however early the women had come to the tomb, it would still have been empty. Matthew admittedly did try to describe what happened. 'There was', he wrote, 'a violent earthquake, for an angel of the Lord came down from heaven and, going to the tomb, rolled back the stone' (28.2). In the apocryphal Gospel of Peter there is an even more vivid description:

> Early in the morning, when the Sabbath dawned, there came a crowd from Jerusalem and the country roundabout to see the sepulchre that had been sealed. Now in the night in which the Lord's day dawned, when the soldiers, two by two in every watch, were keeping guard, there rang out a loud voice in heaven, and they saw the heavens opened and two men come down from there in great brightness and draw nigh to the sepulchre. That stone which had been laid against the entrance to the sepulchre started of itself to roll away and gave way to the side, and the sepulchre was opened, and both the young men entered in (Gospel of Peter 9).

For the other evangelists, it was enough that the tomb was empty. Paul did not mention this tradition. The opponents of the early church did not produce the body but circulated the story that it had been stolen by the disciples.

The tradition seems to have become more physically realistic and external as it developed. The fragmentary nature of the Gospel evidence points to a spiritual experience which was decisive for the disciples. They were changed from frightened men and women to brave witnesses to the Risen Christ. Yet their witness is an invitation to faith and a call to the reader to make their experience his or her own (John 20.30). I find attractive the suggestion that the conclusion to Mark's Gospel was not lost, but that the evangelist intended to end it with the words, 'Trembling and bewildered, the women went out and fled from the tomb. They said nothing to anyone, because they were afraid' (Mark 16.8).[4] The reader of the Gospel, however, knows that the women did speak of the resurrection, but the reader is a member of the believing community. It was not public knowledge.

The Gospels do not argue the evidence for the resurrection. They bear witness and offer a call to faith. This is why the resurrection is not proof of God's activity, but an invitation to trust God.

At the Passover seder, participants are expected to count themselves as among those who escaped from Egypt. In the same way, the resurrection narratives invite the reader to encounter the Risen Lord. As Rowan Williams has said, the experience of Jesus' resurrection was from the first an experience of forgiveness and of the healing of memories of injury, guilt or failure. It was an inner transformation in each believer, not an external event.[5]

The meanings given to the resurrection

With a great painting or poem, there is not one correct meaning, because great art evokes a response in each person. In the same way, different meanings have been put upon the resurrection.

The Gospel narratives, I have suggested, call the reader to a new relationship with God. There is an appropriate air of mystery, because, as many contemporary theologians recognize,[6] the personal encounter with God, present in the Risen Christ, cannot be described in physical, materialistic terms.

It seems that quite soon the Easter story came to be told as an external event and that it became the basis for claims for the divine authority of Jesus. Matthew's Gospel, as we have seen, tried to describe the rolling back of the stone (28.2). In liturgy and hymns, the resurrection became an objective, even cosmic event. As the

Easter liturgy declares, 'This is the night when Jesus Christ vanquished hell and rose triumphant from the grave.'[7]

Still today many Easter hymns, as a few quotations will illustrate, appear to describe an objective event.

> Enclosed he lay in rocky cell,
> With guard of armed sentinel;
> But thence returning, strong and free,
> He comes with pomp of jubilee.[8]

> Engorged in former years, their prey
> Must death and hell restore today;
> And many a captive soul, set free,
> With Jesus leaves captivity.[9]

> On the third day he rose again
> Glorious in majesty to reign.[10]

Another, modern hymn begins by stating, 'It was just two thousand years ago' that an empty tomb was discovered, thus clearly suggesting that the resurrection was a dateable event.[11] Certainly the year in which Jesus was crucified and in which his followers claimed that he had been raised from the dead could, in principle, be given a date – even if that date is disputed. But the binding of the powers of hell or the exaltation of the risen Lord are not similarly dateable historical events.

Another difficulty is that it sometimes seems one can only sing Easter hymns if one is impervious to the horrors of the contemporary world. Indeed, there was a report of a church in Lebanon hit by a rocket just as the celebrant was intoning, 'Christ is Risen; He is Risen indeed.' One admires the courage of that priest and congregation. The Easter faith is indeed that love is stronger than hate; but that is a matter of faith and hope, not of observable reality.

The hymns also link the authority of Jesus to his being raised from the dead. Indeed, Matthew's Gospel ends with the Risen Christ claiming, 'All authority in heaven and on earth has been given to me' (28.18). In the early chapters of the Acts of the Apostles, Peter claimed that:

> God has raised this Jesus to life and we are all witnesses of the fact. Exalted to the right hand of God, he has received from the Father the promised Holy Spirit . . . (2.32).

or

> That he may send the Christ, who has been appointed for you – even Jesus. He must remain in heaven until the time comes for God to restore everything (3.20).

The letter to the Ephesians says:

> He raised Christ from the dead and seated him at his right hand in the heavenly realms far above all authority and rule, power and dominion and every title that can be given, not only in the present age but also in the one to come (Eph. 1.20).

The claim is staggering and one can see how easily it becomes the basis for triumphalistic attitudes. It needs also to be added that talk of the resurrection as a victory (I Cor. 15.25) had dangerous implications. Those who did not believe (John 8.44) were despised as 'children of the devil'. As early as the second century, Irenaeus wrote: 'Those who do not believe in God, and do not do His will, are called sons or angels of the devil, since they do the works of the devil.'[12]

I shall return to the titles of Jesus in a subsequent chapter. My difficulty with traditional language, which is my point here, is that it appears to be objective in describing ultimate reality or the 'court of heaven', whereas for me faith in the Risen Christ is commitment in his strength to seek to follow his self-giving way of life. The tone of traditional language seems to call for a misleading assent to certain metaphysical speculations, whereas the language is pictorial – and many hymns by their use of paradox indicate that their imagery is not to be taken literally. The danger, however, is that by taking it too literally such language can be used as a basis for Christian triumphalism and for scorn of those who do not share the faith.

The meaning of the resurrection for today

To talk of the resurrection and the ascension of Jesus in the language of victory, especially in an apparently objective manner, strikes a jarring note in the shadow of the Shoah – not least because the triumphalistic mood of the Christian church in many centuries directly contributed to the terrible suffering of the Jews.

The Jewish objection to the claim for Christ that the messianic age of peace and justice has evidently not come is justified. To evade this, Christians have sometimes transferred salvation to the next world or interpreted it in individualistic terms as the release of the individual from the sense of sin. The Jewish objection reminds Christians of their daily prayer, 'Thy kingdom come on earth as it is in heaven'. Christians, like Jews, are committed to pray and work for the establishment of God's reign of justice and peace. To assume that God will suddenly put all things right seems an abdication of human responsibility and, after all the genocides of this century, one cannot avoid asking why God has not already acted.

My own belief is that God, in giving human beings freedom, has put into human hands the future of human society. God will not suddenly intervene to put right the mess and horror that we have created. Rather, in Torah and Christ, God has shown us the path of life and gives us strength to be God's partners in the restoration of all things.[13]

The resurrection looks forward to that restoration. It is future in the sense that it confirms the hope that life can be transformed by the self-giving way of life embodied by Jesus. As Rosemary Radford Ruether has written:

> The crucifixion of the Messiah by the unredeemed forces of history cannot be overcome by the proclamation of Easter and then transformed into a secret triumph. Easter gives no licence to vilify those who cannot see it. Indeed, we must see that Easter does not cancel the crucifixion at all. There is no triumph in history. Easter is hope against what remains the continuing reality of the cross.[14]

This is similar to Martin Buber's talk of 'moment gods' – that faith and unfaith are continually struggling with each other. As Rabbi Irving Greenberg has said:

> We have to speak of 'moment faiths', when the redeemer and the vision of redemption are present, interspersed with times when the flames and smoke of the burning children blot out faith – though it flickers again . . . The difference between the sceptic and the believer is the frequency of faith and not the certitude of position . . . Neither Exodus nor Easter wins out nor is totally blotted out by Buchenwald, but we encounter both polar experiences. The life of faith is lived between them.[15]

Easter gives me confidence that the self-giving love shown by Jesus and most vividly expressed upon the cross is the way of life affirmed by God. The certainty is one of faith – a conviction that cannot be the object of external proof – that this is the authentic way of life.

Whatever my own failures, whatever the horrors of the world, in Christ I have been encountered by what is true and by his call to follow him. The stories of Easter and my membership of the Christian church confirm that I am not alone in this conviction, but it is not one that can be demonstrated by events in the world nor by treating Easter as an external historical event. The hope, despite the evidence of the world, that Christ is risen is a trust in the Living God and in God alone. It is, I think, a confidence similar to that of those Jews, who in the midst of life's agonies, continue to wait with faith for the coming of the messianic kingdom. As an unknown Jew wrote on a wall in the besieged Warsaw ghetto:

> I believe, I believe, I believe,
> with a perfect faith
> in the coming of the Messiah;
> and in the coming of the Messiah I believe.
> And even though he tarry
> I nevertheless believe,

Even though he tarry
Yet, I believe in him
I believe, I believe, I believe.[16]

7

'HE HUMBLED HIMSELF'

Jesus, we are told by Paul, 'humbled himself' and took the form of a slave rather than grasping at divine glory. But the history of the church has often been one of arrogant triumphalism, with Christians claiming a monopoly of God's love. They looked down on all 'Jews, Turks, Infidels and Hereticks', even if they occasionally prayed that God would take away from them 'all ignorance, hardness of heart and contempt of Thy word'.[1] At times, Christians tried to force Jews, Muslims and heretics to convert, or slaughtered them with the sword or burnt them at the stake.

The language of worship has often fuelled this triumphalism, picturing Jesus Christ as 'King of Kings and Lord of Lords', who at the end of time would judge all people – sometimes the church presumed to exercise that judgment in advance![2] The emphasis on majesty and the image of victory associated with the resurrection of Jesus also suggests power and defeated enemies.[3] The church needs constantly to be reminded that the power of Christ is the strength of self-giving love and the authority of Christ is the conviction of truth.

In the Fourth Gospel, John intends the reader to see the crucifixion, resurrection and giving of the Spirit as one event. Luke imposed a time sequence on this which, adopted in the church's liturgy, has become part of Christian thinking. Luke's chronology may encourage the tendency to see Easter as a reversal of Good Friday. In John's Gospel, Easter highlights the meaning of the crucifixion. Gerd Lüdemann, from a different standpoint, reaches a similar conclusion, when he writes that his 'historical reconstruction led to the insight that the characteristics of the Easter experience (forgiveness of sins, experience of life, experience of eternity) were already contained in the words and story of Jesus'.[4]

When John speaks of Jesus' death on the cross he uses the phrase 'the glorification of Jesus'. He also uses a Greek word translated as 'lifted up', which is intended to refer both to the fact that Jesus was lifted up on the cross and that he was exalted to God's right hand. For John, it is Jesus' death which is the victory, because here the limitless love of Jesus, which is the limitless love of God, was revealed. Easter added no new revelation to Calvary. It was the moment when the disciples began to understand that the death from which they had fled was not defeat but within the purpose of God. Appropriately, the women who stayed by the cross were the first to see the Risen Lord.

To begin to grasp that God's love in Christ has no limit is to see some traditional Christian teaching from a new perspective. Judgment, as John's Gospel itself says, is not God's punishment, but the misery which humans bring upon themselves by rejecting the way of love (John 3.16–21). Traditional pictures of the Last Things – Death, Judgment, Heaven and Hell – are unsatisfactory. Admittedly, Jesus seems to have used some traditional imagery in his teaching, but this seems to have been to emphasize the urgency of choosing a new way of life. If God's love is universal and unconditional, which is implicit in the love made known in Jesus, then it is a contradiction to suggest that there is a moment when that love is no longer available. To apply time-bound imagery to the life beyond is risky. In my view, universalism, in the sense that all people will in the end be reconciled to God, is implicit in the character of divine love shown on the cross. Such love does not cease loving and offering the opportunity of forgiveness and return. As Desmond Tutu has written in *No Future Without Forgiveness*, 'God does not give up on anyone, for God loved us from all eternity, God loves us now and God will always love us, all of us, good and bad, for ever and ever.'[5] Such love also implies universalism in the sense that God's love is for all people whatever their religious beliefs. Too often Christians have spoken of themselves as 'saved'. This creates a dangerously dualist mentality with a sense that 'we' are better than 'others', who presumably are 'unsaved'. Link this to the imagery of victory – 'kingdom authority flows from His throne unto His own' – and one can see how a perversion of Christian claims has been used to underwrite persecution, inquisition and pogroms.

A limitless love is too threatening. In such forgiving love, all are equal. It erodes our distinctions and privileges and self-importance. This I suppose is why Christians so often discuss whether people of other faiths receive God's salvation. I believe the Christian calling is to witness to the love she or he sees in Jesus Christ. If others testify to similar wonderful apprehensions of the divine, this is a matter for rejoicing, not for jealous competition.

Central to my own discipleship is the experience, in response to the preaching of the cross, of an overwhelming accepting love in which I know myself to be at peace, despite my weakness, depression, sin and failure. It was not a response to a conscious repentance of sin, but an unexpected joy at being loved. For me, in the story of Jesus' passion, I heard the story of a person of radiant goodness who loved without limit, who was willing to forgive those who had caused his death and in whose love I was embraced.

> Here might I stay and sing,
> No story so divine;
> Never was love, dear King,
> Never was grief like thine!
> This is my Friend
> In whose sweet praise
> I all my days
> Could gladly spend.[6]

In that love, I found what for me was the meaning of life. I have tried to understand the world and human relations in the light of that experience and to open my life to be shaped by that love.

It is because of the centrality of that experience to my self-understanding that the love of Jesus has divine authority. In the experiences of total peace in the presence of the divine mystery in nature, I have sensed also a love and acceptance that has no limit.[7]

It is my conviction that in Christ I have been met by 'Very God of

Very God'. Similar experiences have nourished faithful Christians through the centuries. The literature of Christian devotion and of hymnody may well give the best insight into Christian faith. They reflect too the encounter with the Living God which is characteristic of the psalms, which have had a profound influence on Christian hymns. The claims of the creeds are an attempt to affirm this Christian experience.

I see the creeds, however, not as immutable, but as historical documents pointing to the central Christian experience of God's love in Christ. Christian doctrine should be an attempt to understand all life in the light of that experience.

This means that the titles of Jesus are of value in so far as they point people to his forgiving love. They are not of importance in themselves. I recall when studying theology at university, being concerned that the suggestion of biblical critics that Jesus did not call himself Son of God lessened his divine authority. But the titles are not so much about his status as about the impression he has made on those who believe in him. As Raymond Brown put it: 'If Jesus presented Himself as one in whose life God was active, He did so not primarily by the use of titles, or by clear statements about what he was, but rather by the impact of his person and his life on those who followed him.'[8] People in every century have seen a Jesus who is relevant to their time.[9]

The question of which titles Jesus used of himself has been much discussed.[10] This is a historical enquiry and to my mind does not affect the meaning put upon Jesus. Indeed the experience of God's love in Jesus, while deriving from the historical figure, has a certain independence of history. People of influence acquire the meaning put upon them over the centuries. We do not know Jesus' own sense of his destiny and mission. There has been long debate about the significance of the title 'Son of Man'[11] and many scholars question whether Jesus thought of himself as Messiah.[12] It is widely agreed that John's Gospel reflects the meaning that an early Christian community saw in him rather than his own claims. I picture Jesus as having a specially intimate awareness of God's presence and love and being obedient to him in his life and in his death. To me, it is probable that he was conscious of a special vocation and sensed the dangers of the approach to Jerusalem. It may be that he found comfort in the passages in Isaiah about the suffering servant.

When it comes to the developed doctrines of the church, I come to them with the question 'what is the truth of experience?' that those who shaped these doctrines were trying to communicate. Such an approach avoids the conservative's reluctance to question and the modernist's temptation to dismiss the tradition. We are not to presume that we are spiritually wiser than our forefathers.

I have, for example, come to appreciate the depth of meaning in the doctrine of the Trinity. The teaching that the second person of the Trinity is consubstantial with the Father indicates that Jesus was more than a very good and inspiring person. It affirms that in him the believer has encountered true God. Indeed, as I understand it, the doctrine of the Trinity affirms that the one God is met by the believer in the works of creation, in the person of Jesus, and in the spiritual experience of the faithful. The term 'person' in modern English suggests a distinct centre of consciousness which was not the meaning of the Greek term which is translated as person. The Greek word originally meant the mask that an actor wore. The English usage suggests greater division between the three persons of the Trinity than was originally intended. This is why some Jews and Muslims feel that Christianity comes too close to tritheism and compromises pure monotheism.[13] Yet the doctrine of the Trinity is not just about how God is apprehended by humans. It is intended also to say something about the being of God. It reflects the Christian conviction that God is in essence Love – the mutual Love of the Father and the Son through the Holy Spirit. The world is not necessary to God so that God should have someone to love and by whom to be loved. God's very nature is love. The image of the Trinity also suggests dynamism and development whereas talk of 'the Alone' can appear static.

I am not suggesting that the doctrine can describe the Godhead in its own being. Rather that certain images, despite their inadequacy, are more adequate than others. As Ninian Smart wrote some years ago with reference to the Hindu tendency to say that all religions are really the same: 'God is not literally a Father, nor Durga literally a Mother. But this is no argument. God is not literally a Father, but in Christian theology He is not even non-literally an onion. Some expressions are more appropriate than others'.[14] I appreciate the limitations of speaking of God as Father, not just to those who would prefer to speak of God as Mother, but also to those who would prefer to speak of the Absolute. Yet for me the term 'Absolute' does not suggest the possibility of personal communion with the Ultimate.

In the same way, astonishing as is the doctrine of the incarnation, if God wishes to be in communication with human beings it makes sense to me that the fullest relationship is established in and through a human being. In human relationships we can communicate by letter or telephone or today by fax or email, but there is no substitute for personal meeting and conversation. Equally often we are not satisfied with a secretary or a receptionist. We want to meet the person in charge. The doctrine of the incarnation suggests that God is revealed to us in the most intimate way possible and that in the person of Jesus we are met by God and not by a lesser being.

The teaching that the Christ was pre-existent and that he was incarnated and born of a virgin are to me ways of affirming the presence of God in Jesus. They grow out of the believer's experience. It is interesting to compare the developments of buddhology in Mahayana Buddhism with the developments of christology and of the Logos doctrine in Christianity. If the Eternal is encountered in a human being then that being is inherently eternal and has existed for all time.

An emphasis on the eternal glory of Christ, however, may seem to increase the distance between Christianity and Judaism and Islam. I do not, however, think that is necessary. Titles which affirm Christ's high dignity should be seen to grow from the believer's conviction that in Christ he or she has been met by God and has known the healing peace of the divine. The titles given to Jesus are an expression of the Christian community's experience of God. The question then to discuss with Jewish and Muslim friends is whether their experience of God is similar. Is their deepest religious experience one in which they have been encountered by God? Is the God so encountered to be spoken of in personal terms? Is the experience one of peace and forgiveness and wholeness? How is the experience of the Eternal mediated to human beings caught up in a changing world? However much Jews and Muslims affirm the monotheism of God, do they speak of a mediating principle and is it appropriate to apply personal language to that mediating principle? It has often been observed that the book of Proverbs applies personal language to Wisdom in a way similar to that applied in the New Testament to the Logos (Prov. 8) and that some rabbis symbolized Torah in a personal form.[16]

We have I feel hardly begun to ask in our interfaith dialogue about the experience that lies beneath our traditions. I recognize the difficulty of this and a natural reluctance to speak of our most intimate and private spiritual experiences. Only, however, as we do this shall we discover how close or far apart we are.

In this context, my concern is whether my affirmation of the experience of God's graciousness in Jesus Christ – and the doctrinal edifice built upon it – does at least make sense to my Jewish or Muslim friend. Does he or she recognize the experience of which I am speaking? Does it have any resonances in other traditions? If so, is it possible for me to affirm my experience and remain loyal to the inheritance of my faith community without at the same time denigrating the faith traditions of the Jewish people?

Various considerations may help to prevent an affirmation of the Lordship of the Risen Christ being heard in an anti-Jewish way.

The first is to make clear that Jesus was a faithful son of the covenant and loyal to the Torah. Dr Jacobus Schoneveld, a former General Secretary of the International Council of Christians and Jews, for example, says, 'the resurrection means the vindication of Jesus as a Jew, as a person who was faithful to the Torah, as a martyr who participated in Jewish martyrdom for the sanctification of God's Name. What else can this mean than the validation of the Torah and vindication of the Jewish people as God's beloved people?'[17] Jesus fulfilled the Torah by his radical obedience to the Father. This meant that it was sufficient for Paul to tell his Gentile converts to be followers or imitators of Jesus. For if Jesus was obedient to the Torah, then those who imitated Jesus would be obeying the spirit, if not the letter, of Torah.

Although Jews at the time of Jesus were divided on whether or not they believed in resurrection, it was commonly held that God would raise the righteous martyr (Dan. 12.2–3). It has to be remembered that it was Jews who affirmed that Jesus had been raised, Jews who declared he was Messiah and Lord. The Orthodox Jew, Dr Pinchas Lapide, in his book *The Resurrection of Jesus*, writes: 'From a rabbinic point of view the resurrection is basically a messianic Midrash of the first community of Jesus which grew out of the confidence in God's loving righteousness and of the faith in Jesus as the proclaimer of salvation who was sent by God.'[18]

Another Jewish scholar, Alan Segal, writes: 'Jesus ascends to heaven because astral immortality is promised to those martyrs who make others wise, and Jesus is pre-eminently a martyr.'[19] The resurrection of Jesus may be seen in Jewish terms as the vindication of a holy martyr.

There was nothing un-Jewish in thinking that a great man had been signally honoured by God in being taken up to heaven, in being given a role in the final judgment of the world and in being recognized as Messiah or Son of God. To the first believers, the term 'Son of God' probably implied Jesus' moral obedience to the Father. James Dunn argues that to call Jesus 'Lord' was evidently not understood in earliest Christianity as identifying him with God. What Paul and the first Christians seem to have done was to claim that the one God had shared his lordship with the exalted Christ.'[20]

Paul in I Corinthians 8.6 and in Colossians 1.15–20 (if Colossians is by Paul himself) applied to Jesus language elsewhere applied to divine Wisdom. By identifying Jesus with the figure of divine Wisdom, Paul may have introduced ideas of pre-existence and of Jesus' role in the creation of the world. Wisdom is called 'an image of God's goodness' (Wisd. 7.26) and she is said to have been created by the Lord 'at the beginning of his work' (Prov. 8.22). In Colossians it is said that Christ 'is the image of the invisible God, the first born of all creation' (Col. 1.15). Dunn contends that Jews at that time did not think of Wisdom as a separate divine being, but as a way of expressing God's self-revelation. Jewish monotheism was 'so confident of its major premise that (it could) speak vigorously of God's wisdom without any thought of attributing a separate divine status to this wisdom or of compromising that monotheism'.[21] It is likely that Paul in applying the language previously used of Wisdom to the figure of Christ used it in the same sense, without implying that he was a separate divine being.

It is the same when Paul speaks of the glory of God being made visible in Jesus Christ. Paul claims that it was the glory of God which shone in the face of Jesus Christ (II Cor. 4.6; cf. John 1.14). 'There was in the Bible', writes Alan Segal, 'a human theophany, a human appearance of God, often called the angel of the Lord but also called the Kavod, God's Glory, or even once the Son of man, as in Daniel. By the time of Jesus, these peculiar notions could be combined into a single, divine, human figure who carries or embodies the name of God. The best shorthand way to explain what the scriptural interpretations make of this figure is to call it God's principal angel, because that's what we call human manifestations of God in heaven. But this angel is not merely one of God's creatures. It is this figure whom the Christians identified as Jesus, thus making the Christ and the Lord one.'[22] Likewise, the term *Shekinah* speaks of theophany; of an overwhelming experience of God's presence.

John like Paul uses the term glory, saying in the Prologue to his Gospel, that 'the Word became flesh; he came to dwell among us, and we saw his glory, such glory as befits the Father's only Son, full of grace and truth (John 1.14). Several recent studies suggest that the Fourth Gospel comes from a Jewish milieu. James Dunn suggests that the Johannine community believed its claims for Jesus were compatible with Jewish monotheism. For John, '*Jesus is the Wisdom-Logos of God, that is, the self-revelation of God himself.* To have seen him *is* to have seen the Father. In other words, *John saw himself still as a monotheist*; he understands what he was saying about Jesus Christ as *still within the bounds of Jewish monotheism*. This is why it would be wholly accurate at this point to sum up his Christology thus: For John, Jesus was the incarnation not of the Son of God but of God – God's self-revelation become flesh and blood.'[23] For the

Jewish leaders, however, John had gone too far: but the partings of the ways were historically conditioned rather than theologically inevitable. Christians and Jews, therefore, need not be imprisoned by their tragic history. This is why it is not just wishful thinking to suggest we could answer 'yes' to the question put by the Roman Catholic writer Andrew Greeley when he asked, 'Could we eventually arrive at a Christology with which both Jews and Catholics could live? Not now, surely, not for a long time, but maybe, if we begin to talk about what we do share now, sometime?'[24]

The parting became set in concrete as the church's membership became predominantly Gentile. 'This is really where the serious and apparently intractable difficulties in Christology begin,' wrote Monika Hellwig, 'in a simplification in Gentile context and language of the elusive Hebrew way of speaking about the mystery of God and of God's dealings with creation and history'.[25]

Any hesitation about speaking directly of Jesus Christ as God soon disappeared. Ignatius of Antioch, for example, ended his letter to the Romans by sending 'abundant greetings of unalloyed joy in Jesus Christ our God'.[26] Ignatius could also speak of 'the suffering of my God' or say that 'God . . . was conceived by Mary'.[27]

The general approach in the second century was to think that the pre-existent Christ-Spirit either indwelt the man Jesus or actually became man. Justin Martyr said that 'he who was formerly the Logos, and appeared now in the semblance of fire, now in incorporeal fashion, has finally by God's will become man for the human race'.[28] Irenaeus insisted that divine Word entered fully into human life. Athenagoras of Athens, in trying to explain the incarnation to Greek intellectuals, insisted on the absolute unity and spirituality of God. He then asked whether the claim that God had a son was intelligible. He suggested, by an allusion to Greek philosophy, that it was intelligible if the sonship is understood not as biological sonship but as of a being who was begotten of a thought or utterance. The notion of 'logos' as the mediating principle between the utterly inaccessible ultimate One and the world of plurality and contingency was familiar.[29]

It could be said of second-century christology that Christ was still the incarnate Logos, God's revelation become flesh and blood. Christ was not yet the third person of the Trinity. The change began to happen in the writings of Origen. In his *Peri Archon* or *De Principiis*, the identity of Jesus is established in the eternally pre-existing Word before any account is presented of Jesus in history. 'We believe', he wrote, 'that the very Logos of the Father, the Wisdom of God Himself, was enclosed within the limits of the man that appeared in Judaea; nay more, that God's Wisdom entered a woman's womb, was born as an infant, and wailed like crying children.'[30] He explained this by reference to his belief that all spiritual beings, including human souls, were pre-existent from all eternity. One of these souls, the one destined to be the soul of the man Jesus, in every respect a human like the rest, was from the beginning attached to the Logos with mystical devotion; it burned with love and desire for justice. All other souls, by the misguided exercise of their free will, fell away from the Logos to whom they ought to have adhered, but this unique soul, as a result of its adoring contemplation, became inseparably united with the Logos. The union, Origen said, was as complete as that of a lump of iron with the fire into which it is plunged.[31] For Origen, only God the Father is in the strict sense God. Jesus Christ is God in a subordinate sense. The church later rejected this view, just as it also discarded his belief that all souls were pre-existent. The church did, however, retain the vocabulary of three Persons or *hypostases*, which Origen seems to have been the first to use. But the church came to give the term a different meaning.

The Greek term *hypostasis* was translated into Latin by Tertullian as *persona*. But the English term 'person', which suggests an individual self-conscious being, is, as already mentioned, a misleading translation for *persona*. As Monika Hellwig puts it: 'The modern concept of person as an individual reflexive self-awareness and centre of spontaneity is simply not what was intended by the term either when Tertullian introduced it or when the Councils adopted it in defining orthodoxy.'[32]

The point I have been trying to make is that until the third century the emphasis was on the unity of the Godhead and that Jesus

Christ was the revelation of God in a human life. Such a view was not entirely alien to the more speculative Jewish thinking of the first century, although with the ascendancy of rabbinic Judaism, such speculation was frowned upon. Just as Christian and Jewish scholars, recognizing that the first-century partings of the ways was a gradual process determined partly by contingent historical events, look at those developments without the inherited bitterness, so it may be possible to see that christological developments were not inevitable and that the Christian experience of God's presence in Christ could have been expressed in other terms. The development of trinitarian theology increased the gulf between Jews and Christians and also is a major cause of separation between Christians and Muslims. The time has come to re-examine the development of this doctrine to see if there is a way by which Christians can affirm God's presence in Christ without so separating themselves from their Abrahamic brothers and sisters. It has also to be said that some Christians for other reasons find the traditional picture of God coming down to earth hard to comprehend and now speak of the doctrine of the incarnation as a myth.[33] This, however, provokes a strong reaction from those who look to the authority of the creeds to shore up the church's traditional expression of its faith.

Creedal fundamentalism

Sadly, a creedal fundamentalism seems to have replaced biblical fundamentalism in many churches. Despite the work of significant scholars in this field, willingness to say the creeds – even if they are not understood – seems in many congregations to be the touchstone of orthodoxy. To question the creeds, as the Catholic writer Gregory Baum wrote some years ago, is too threatening. 'It is at this point that some Christian theologians get "cold feet". They fear that a radical reinterpretation of the Church's central doctrine might dissolve the gospel altogether.'[34] Monika Hellwig agrees that 'there is a common reluctance to face the more fundamental question of whether the enterprise of the great councils was flawed in its intellectual conception'. She suggests that the very attempt to define the divine nature was mistaken because it ignored the necessary mystery of all language about the divine:

> The biblical and intertestamentary heritage common to Christians and Jews involved a respect for mystery – and an intellectual humility before it – which was largely implicit. The judicious use of narrative, symbolism, discreet allusion, paradox, and so forth, was an implicit acknowledgment of the nature and limitations of religious language and of faith assertions. The Christian option for Greek philosophical categories in patristic times and for intensively philosophical systematization of the religious heritage in mediaeval times did much to weaken that acknowledgment. But modern philosophy itself has taken relentless (one might say merciless) note of the nature and limitation of all language, the relation of religious language to truth claims and the role of symbol in human understanding and expression.[36]

Rethinking christology

To communicate the mystery of God's presence in Jesus Christ today may mean starting again, as the language of the creeds may be a hindrance rather than a help. The whole concept of the pre-existent Christ and of the virgin birth may be rich in mythological significance, but for a growing number of Christians today this is the language of poetry not of 'fact'. Indeed many Liberal Christians start with the human Jesus, not with the God who becomes man, and see in his life and ministry, death and resurrection the clue to the character of God. This approach is often summed up in the words of Paul that 'God was in Christ'. As the Catholic John Pawlikowski has said, 'our attitude toward the statement "Jesus is Son of God" and "Jesus is divine"' needs to change from 'simple quotation to interpretation'.[37] The philosopher John Hick, with a different approach to the subject, has also written: 'It seems reasonable to conclude that the real point and value of incarnational doctrine is not indicative but expressive, not to assert a metaphysical fact but to express a valuation and evoke an attitude.'[38] This seems more in tune with what the first disciples are likely to have meant when they called Jesus 'Son of God' than some of the language of the creeds.

It is the living experience of faith behind the formularies that we need to discover. True Christian continuity is in sharing that experience, not in repeating ancient catch-phrases. We can affirm the reality of being met by God in Jesus Christ without a particular time-bound metaphysic.

There are significant differences both between Christianity and Judaism and within both faiths, but in our deepest beliefs about the nature of God, we are close together. Jesus brings his followers to the God of Abraham, Isaac and Jacob. The ways, therefore, in which Christians express their faith in Jesus Christ should affirm the links with Judaism, rather than the reverse.

8

PAUL

If it is true that Jesus brings Christians to the God of Abraham, Isaac and Jacob, then any suggestion that Christianity has superseded or replaced Judaism has to be repudiated. Yet, for centuries, the church has claimed that it has inherited the promises which God made to Israel, as God had abandoned the Jewish people.

The argument centres on Paul's writings. From a Jewish perspective, Paul has been seen as an apostate, who said that Judaism with its observance of the Law was inferior to Gentile Christianity with its faith in Christ.[1] Many Christians would agree, except to them Paul was a hero, establishing a new covenant people to replace the 'old' Israel. Yet, there are good reasons to question traditional interpretations of Paul's life and teachings. The matter is very complex, partly because of a range of interlocking issues on which there is little agreement among scholars. For example, did Paul reject the Torah or did he still observe it? Was his key concern how to be justified with God or how to win Gentiles to faith in Christ Jesus? Did he think God's covenant with Israel was still effective or had it been cancelled? These are still controversial questions

'The phrase "Paul and Judaism"', writes E. P. Sanders at the beginning of his six hundred-page *Paul and Palestinian Judaism*, 'starts more questions than can be dealt with in one book'.[2] It is perhaps an act of folly and hubris, therefore, to hope to deal with this subject in a chapter, but the interpretation of Paul has still today a significant bearing on Christian–Jewish relations. There are those who quote Paul to justify missionary attempts to convert Jews to Christianity, and those who enlist his support for a ban on such conversionist activity. Since the Holocaust he has often been blamed for the anti-

Semitism and anti-Judaism of the church, but some scholars have reinterpreted his teaching to clear him of this charge. Recently, however, it has been suggested that this reinterpretation is itself distorted by a predetermined agenda to clear Paul of anti-Semitism. 'The whole post-Auschwitz determination to discover "anti-Judaism" under every possible New Testament bush is no doubt a necessary reaction to the anti-Judaism endemic in much previous New Testament scholarship, but at the moment it is, frankly, shedding just as much darkness on serious historical understanding as did its predecessor,' writes the Anglican scholar Tom Wright.[3]

Grace not works

The traditional Protestant view has been that Paul, after his conversion, preached that a person could only be saved through faith in Jesus Christ and his redeeming death. Paul, according to this view, rejected Judaism, because it taught that a person could only win acceptance with God ('justification') by good works.

This view goes back to the highly influential exposition by the reformer Martin Luther (1483–1546), for whom 'justification by faith is the principal doctrine of Christianity'.[4] Luther opposed this teaching to the Jewish attempt to earn justification by works of the Law. In his lectures on Galatians, he commented on Galatians 3.10, saying: 'To be justified by works of the Law is to deny the righteousness of faith . . . The righteousness of the Law which they [the Jews] think they are producing is in fact nothing but idolatry and blasphemy against God.'[5] Like the Jews, the world, the devil and the pope wrongly believed that God's approval could be won by a person's own righteousness. But, as even keeping the Law of God could not earn justification, even less could human works do so. 'We are justified', wrote Luther, 'neither by the righteousness of the Law nor by our own righteousness but solely by faith in Christ.'[6]

Among the arguments Luther used to support his position was his own experience as a monk. However meticulous he was in seeking to obey God's demands, he could not achieve inner peace. He wrote:

When I was a monk, I made a great effort to live according to the requirements of the monastic rule . . . Nevertheless, my conscience could never achieve certainty but was always in doubt and said: 'You have not done this correctly. You were not contrite enough. You omitted this in your confession.' Therefore the longer I tried to heal my uncertain, weak, and troubled conscience with human traditions, the more uncertain, weak and troubled I continually made it.[7]

When Paul wrote 'I find this Law at work. When I want to do good, evil is right there with me. For in my inner being I delight in God's Law, but I see another Law at work in the members of my body waging war against the Law of my mind and making me a prisoner of the Law of sin at work within my members,' Luther thought Paul was describing the same experience. By interpreting Romans 7 as an autobiographical memoir by Paul, Luther concluded that Judaism was a matter of trying to earn justification by good works.

Today many scholars reject this autobiographical interpretation of Romans 7. Following W. G. Kümmel, they think Paul was using the first person rhetorically to picture the lot of humanity under the Law. Either interpretation, however, is likely to suggests a negative view of the Law, although Stephen Westerholm thinks that Paul's argument was intended to be in defence of the Law.[8]

This misleading contrast between righteousness by works (Judaism) and righteousness by grace (Christianity) was said by Luther to reflect the teaching of Augustine. It is a contrast that has been used in the twentieth century to distinguish the gospel – an act of God – from all religion, which has been described as a human striving for God.[9]

This contrast is to be found in well-known hymns such as Augustus Toplady's (1740–78) 'Rock of Ages', with these words,

> Not the labours of my hands
> Can fulfil thy Law's demands;
> Could my zeal no respite know,
> Could my tears for ever flow,

> All for sin could not atone:
> Thou must save, and thou alone.[10]

The same attitude is still to be found in writers of the twentieth century. For example, the influential New Testament scholar Rudolf Bultmann wrote:

> The contrast between Paul and Judaism consists not merely in his assertion of the present reality of righteousness, but also in a much more decisive thesis – the one which concerns the condition to which God's acquitting decision is tied. The Jew takes it for granted that this condition is keeping the Law, the accomplishing of works prescribed by the Law. In direct contrast to this view Paul's thesis runs – to consider its negative aspect first: '*without works of the Law*' . . . The negative aspect of Paul's thesis does not stand alone; a positive statement takes its place beside it: '*by, or from, faith*'. [11]

Whatever the religious experience of Martin Luther, there are good reasons to question whether it is right to impose that experience on to the writings of Paul, partly because it misrepresents Jewish teaching and partly because it distorts the central concerns of Paul.

Jewish teaching about the Law

Judaism, as we have already argued,[12] is not a religion of works, but like Christianity a religion of covenant and divine grace. 'Both Judaism and Christianity affirm that a person gains a right relationship with God by being in God's covenant. Correct behaviour is the appropriate response of a person who is in a covenant relationship with God,' writes the Jewish scholar Lester Dean and the Catholic Professor Gerard Sloyan agrees with him.[13]

Jewish writers were the first to insist that the traditional Protestant view of Judaism was mistaken. In 1909, the historian Solomon Schechter (c. 1850–1918) argued that the Greek word *nomos* – translated into English as 'Law' – did not convey the full meaning of the Hebrew word *Torah*. 'The legalistic element, which might rightly be called the Law, represents only one side of the Torah. To the Jew the word Torah means a teaching or an instruction of any kind.'[14]

In 1914, the Liberal Jewish scholar C. G. Montefiore argued that Paul's negative statements about the Law in no way represented rabbinic Judaism. Montefiore claimed that in rabbinic Judaism and also in the teaching of Jesus, 'God was so good and near and kind, and man, through the Law and through repentance, had such constant, easy and efficacious opportunities of access to him, that there was no need of a tremendous cosmic and divine event such as was provided by the incarnation and crucifixion'.[15] Montefiore added:

> And even from sin and misery there was a way out. That way was constructed by God's forgiveness and man's repentance. Its outward symbol was the Day of Atonement. What neither God nor man could do according to Paul except by the incarnation of the Son, was done according to Rabbinic Judaism constantly, hour by hour, year by year. Nothing is more peculiar in the great Epistles than the almost complete omission of the twin Rabbinic ideas of repentance and forgiveness.[16]

Another Jewish scholar, H. J. Schoeps, Professor of the History of Religion at Erlangen, in his book *Paul* (1959), argued that Paul failed to recognize that 'in the Biblical view the Law is integral to the covenant . . . It was given in order to bind the Israelite people to its covenant God as his peculiar possession.' When, however, Paul speaks of the Jewish *nomos,* he implies a twofold curtailment. 'In the first place he has reduced the Torah, which means for the Jews both Law and teaching, to the ethical (and ritual) Law; secondly, he has wrested and isolated the Law from the controlling context of God's covenant with Israel.'[17]

Slowly, too, a few Christian scholars, as mentioned in the second chapter, came to recognize that the description of rabbinic Judaism as a system of earning righteousness by obeying the Law was a gross distortion. The Unitarian Robert Travers Herford (1860–1905) wrote many works on the Talmud. In the 1920s, George Foot Moore (1851–1931) of Harvard University published his three-volume *Judaism in the First Centuries of the Christian Era*. He wrote:

> How a Jew of Paul's antecedents could ignore, and by implication deny, the great prophetic doctrine of repentance, which, individualized and interiorized, was a cardinal doctrine of Judaism, namely that God out of love, freely forgives the sincerely penitent sinner and restores him to his favour – that seems from the Jewish point of view inexplicable.[18]

A few years later, the Anglican scholar James Parkes said that 'if it is Rabbinic Judaism which he [Paul] is attacking, then to a large extent his charges against the Law are unjustified'.[19]

It was, nevertheless, the works of E. P. Sanders that helped to change the consensus view of Christian scholars and led many of them to recognize that Judaism of the first century remained a religion based on God's gracious covenant with the people of Israel, to whom God had given the Torah to be a delight and a joy (Ps. 119). Sanders described Judaism as 'covenantal nomism'.[20]

Was Paul's view of Judaism mistaken?

If first-century Judaism was indeed a form of 'covenantal nomism', why did Paul so misunderstand the religion in which he was brought up – or have scholars misunderstood Paul?

One suggestion has been that Paul had a distorted knowledge of Judaism – probably derived from the Hellenistic Judaism of the Diaspora. But that denies Paul's own testimony that he was a 'Pharisee of the Pharisees' (Phil. 3.5; cf. Acts 26.5). Besides, there is no real evidence that the Judaism of Palestine and of the Diaspora were significantly different.

Another view is that Paul believed that in the new age that had dawned with the coming of Jesus Christ, the Law's efficacy had ceased. E. P. Sanders, for example, towards the end of his *Paul and Palestinian Judaism*, says: 'In short, *this is what Paul finds wrong in Judaism: it is not Christianity.*'[21] Paul, Sanders says, '*in fact explicitly denies that the Jewish covenant can be effective for salvation, thus consciously denying the basis of Judaism'.*[22]

W. D. Davies said much the same but in a way that is more sympathetic to Judaism:

> Both in his life and thought, therefore, Paul's close relation to Rabbinic Judaism has become clear, and we cannot too strongly insist again that for him the acceptance of the Gospel was not so much the rejection of the old Judaism and the discovery of a new religion wholly antithetical to it, as his polemics might sometimes pardonably lead us to assume, but the recognition of the advent of the true and final form of Judaism, in other words, the advent of the Messianic Age of Jewish expectation. It is in this light that we are to understand the conversion of Paul . . . It was not the inadequacy of Judaism . . . that accounts for Paul's conversion, but the impact of the new factor that entered into his ken when he encountered Christ. It was at this one point that Paul parted company with Judaism, at the valuation of Jesus of Nazareth as the Messiah with all that this implied.[23]

Sanders and Davies, however, may over-emphasize both the discontinuity between Paul's pharisaic Judaism and his new faith in Christ Jesus and his eschatological emphasis.

More important, 'justification by faith' was probably not Paul's primary concern.[24] The key issue for Paul appears not to have been the question of how is a person to be justified before God, but on what terms were Gentiles to be admitted to the Christian community. Did those Gentiles who came to faith in Christ have to convert to Judaism, which for men would have involved circumcision, in order to become a member of the covenant people of God? It is in this context that Paul's discussion of the Law is best understood.

William Wrede, whose *Paul* was published in 1908, was one of the first scholars to argue that the question of justification was not Paul's central concern. Wrede stressed the difference between the world view of Paul and his contemporaries and that of people of the twentieth century. For Paul, the 'spirits and superhuman powers' and 'the forces of the universe' (Rom. 8.38) were realties, not abstractions. Soon afterwards, Albert Schweitzer agreed that Paul had to be seen as a man of the first century. He insisted that Paul had to be understood in the context of Jewish eschatology.[25] Paul, Schweitzer argued, shared Jesus' expectation that the cataclysmic end of the world was at hand and was about to be replaced by God's kingdom, at which time Jesus would return to complete his work of redemption. In this new age, already begun by the resurrection of Jesus, the Law's validity would come to an end. Paul and Judaism went in opposite directions. Paul 'sacrificed the Law to eschatology; Judaism abandoned eschatology and retained the Law'.[26]

Some Jews seem to have expected that in the last days Gentiles, or at least some of them, would turn to God. 'These are the words of the Lord of Hosts,' said the prophet Zechariah. 'Nations and dwellers in great cities shall yet come; people of one city shall come to those of another and say, "Let us go and entreat the favour of the Lord, and resort to the Lord of Hosts and I will come too"' (Zech. 8.8, 20–21). In the Psalm of Solomon, which dates to before the fall of Jerusalem in 70 CE, there is the prediction that the nations, despite their defeat and their submission, 'shall come from the ends of the earth to see his [God's] glory, bringing as gifts her sons who had fainted and to see the glory of the Lord (17.34). Even after the fall of Jerusalem and the failure of the Jewish revolts, many rabbis believed that the righteous of the nations would have a share in the life to come.[27]

In the first century, there was an Jewish active mission to the Gentiles and many of them were attracted to the monotheism and high ethical teaching of Judaism.[28] Paul too, although in the early chapters of Romans he shows a low opinion of Gentiles, believed that they could turn to the God of Israel and be saved. Sanders, therefore, from the admittedly scanty evidence, concludes that 'very likely the general expectation of Gentile conversion at the end was common'.[29]

This helps to explain why Paul's 'conversion' was at the same time a commission to preach to the Gentiles. Indeed Krister Stendahl has argued that Paul's experience on the road to Damascus was not so much a 'conversion' as a 'call'. Writing to the Galatians, Paul said, 'God, who set me apart from birth and called me by his grace, was pleased to reveal his Son in me so that I might preach him among the Gentiles' (Gal. 1.15–16; cf. Acts 9.15; 22.15; 26.17).

On what terms could Gentiles join the church?

Paul's preaching to the Gentiles met with considerable success, especially among the 'God-fearers' (Acts 17.4; 13.26). At once this raised questions about what was required of those who wished to become members of the Christian community. Did they have to convert to Judaism as well as confess their faith in Christ Jesus? In part, this was a practical question, because observant Jews, in obedience to the rules of kosher, would only eat with other Jews. Jews and Gentiles did not have table fellowship and presumably could not share together at the Lord's table. This, as Paul says in the Letter to the Galatians, created difficulties and led to a confrontation with Peter.

> When Peter came to Antioch, I opposed him to his face, because he was clearly in the wrong. Before certain men came from James, he used to eat with the Gentiles. But when they arrived, he began to draw back and separate himself from the Gentiles because he was afraid of those who belonged to the circumcision group. The other Jews joined him in this hypocrisy, so that by their hypocrisy even Barnabas was led astray. When I saw that they were not acting in line with the truth of the gospel, I said to Peter in front of them all, 'You are a Jew, yet you live like a Gentile and not like a Jew. How is it that you force Gentiles to follow Jewish customs? We who are Jews by birth and not Gentile sinners know that a man is not justified by observing the Law, but by faith in Jesus Christ. So we, too, have put our faith in Christ Jesus that we may be justified by faith in Christ and not by observing the Law, because by observing the Law no one will be justified' (Gal. 2.11–16).

In the Acts of the Apostles – the historical reliability of which is open to question – there is an account of the dream that Peter had while he was staying at Joppa. He was hungry and while he was waiting for the meal to be prepared, Peter fell asleep. In his dream, he saw heaven opened and something like a large sheet being let down to earth by its four corners. It contained all kinds of four-footed animals, as well as reptiles of the earth and birds of the air. Then a voice told him, 'Get up, Peter. Kill and eat.' 'Surely not, Lord,' Peter replied. 'I have never eaten anything impure or unclean' (Acts 10.11–14). But a voice replied, 'Do not call anything impure that God has made clean.' When Peter woke up, he found waiting for him servants who had been sent to him by the Gentile centurion Cornelius. Peter went with them to Cornelius at Caesarea and while Peter was talking with Cornelius the Holy Spirit came upon the Gentiles, so Peter proceeded to baptize them. Acts insists that the admission of Gentiles to the Christian community was in direct response to the prompting of God.

For Jews to eat with Gentiles raised questions both about whether Jewish believers in Jesus had to observe the Law and whether similar requirements were to be demanded of Gentile believers.

Acts tells us that the first Christians in Jerusalem met daily in the temple courts (Acts 2.46). They continued to be faithful in observance of the Law. When they heard that some Gentiles had become believers, there were those who insisted that these Gentile believers had to do the same. 'Some of the believers who belong to the party of the Pharisees stood up and said, "The Gentiles must be circumcised and required to obey the Law of Moses"' (Acts 15.5). The so-called Council of Jerusalem did not, however, insist on this. It only required Gentiles 'to abstain from food polluted by idols, from sexual immorality, from the meat of strangled animals and from blood' (Acts 15.20).

Developments in the early church are uncertain and much debated. Luke's account and Paul's own letters often disagree. It seems that some Jewish believers in Jesus insisted that Gentile believers had to be converted to Judaism. When they tried to persuade some of Paul's new Gentile converts to follow this course, Paul vigorously opposed them. It is in this context that his attack on the Law, especially in the letter to the Galatians, is to be understood. Paul is not attacking the Law, *per se*, but its imposition on Gentile believers. His concern, as Bishop Krister Stendahl put it, was to show that 'Gentiles must not, and should not, come to Christ *via* the Law.'[30] Similarly, the American scholar John Gager in his important book *The Origins of Anti-Semitism* says of Paul's letter to the Galatians that 'Jews and Judaism are nowhere in the picture. Judaizing, not Judaism, is the issue . . . Paul's sole concern is to defend the status of his Gentile converts as sons of Abraham without first becoming Jews.'[31]

Why then did God give the Law?

In explaining why obedience to the Law was not required of Gentile believers, Paul made clear that he was not denying the sanctity of the Law. He stressed that justification is a matter of faith, not works. He argued that to insist as his opponents did that circumcision *was* essential to a trusting relationship in God was to make justification dependent on an outward ceremony or 'work'. It seems that from the time of the Maccabees, there was an increasing emphasis on circumcision as a sign of Jewish identity. The book of Jubilees says:

> Every one that is born, the flesh of whose foreskin is not circumcised on the eighth day, belongs not to the children of the covenant which the Lord made with Abraham, but to the children of destruction; nor is there, moreover, any sign on him that he is the Lord's, but (he is destined) to be destroyed.[32]

Jewish teaching usually sees circumcision as a sign of the covenant, not as a condition for membership of it. Paul implied that his opponents' position was not in line with Jewish teaching at its best and made circumcision, not faith, the basis for acceptance by God. But, as he says, 'God in his grace gave it [the inheritance] to Abraham through a promise' (Gal. 3.18).

There are indeed very negative remarks about the Law in Galatians, but the point Paul seems to be making is that were a person to be justified by obedience to the Law then that would require of him *total* obedience to the Law. He quotes, to support this claim, a verse from Deuteronomy that says, 'Cursed is everyone who does not continue to do everything written in the Book of the Law' (Gal. 3.10; cf. Deut. 27.26). Clearly nobody is so completely obedient to the Law. Rather, quoting Habbakuk 2.4, Paul insists that 'The righteous will live by faith' (Gal. 3.11). Paul is *not* suggesting that Jews believed they would only be accepted by God if they obeyed every letter of the Law. Rather, Paul assumed that his reader would agree with him that such total obedience was not possible and that the reader too would recognize that acceptance by God was a matter of faith. Paul seems to be appealing to what Sanders calls 'covenantal nomism', which was generally accepted by his Jewish contemporaries. Like them, Paul recognizes that the Law is given in the context of the covenant, which precedes it, and that the faithful are dependent on the mercy of God not on their own sinlessness. Paul is trying to show the impossible position to which the arguments of his opponents, if pushed to the extreme, will lead.

Paul also makes the point that God's covenant with Abraham was based on a promise and that even a human covenant once made cannot be set aside. As the Law was given 430 years after the covenant with Abraham, it does not set aside the promise made to Abraham. Further, because the Law was given years after the covenant, it could not be claimed that it represented God's universal law for all humanity.[33]

Having insisted that acceptance by God is not based on obedience to the Law, Paul makes clear that he is not undermining the significance of the Law. 'Is the Law, therefore, opposed to the promises of God? Absolutely not!" (Gal. 3.12). The Law was indeed a path to righteousness, but because of human disobedience, it in fact made clear 'that the whole world is a prisoner of sin' (Gal. 3.22). The Law was like a slave, whose task it was to take care of a child to and from school. 'The Law was put in charge to lead us to Christ that we might be justified by faith' (Gal. 3.24). It may be that Paul took a more pessimistic view of human nature than was common among his Jewish contemporaries. Certainly, over the centuries, Christians have developed a doctrine of original sin which is not part of Jewish teaching.

Lester Dean, a Jewish scholar, clearly explains the Jewish under-standing of the relationship of Covenant and Law:

> Although Jews do try to observe Torah, their observance of the Law does not mean that Jews are trying to 'work their way into heaven'. A Jew's relationship to God is based upon God's covenant established with the Israelites and their descendants. Jews believe that this covenant is a covenant of grace, just as Christians believe the covenant of the 'New Testament' is a covenant of grace. Both the Hebrew scriptures and rabbinic literature affirm that the Jews did nothing to earn this relation-ship with God, it was God's choice. Thus a Jew's righteousness does not come from observance of Torah; it comes from being a part of God's covenant people.
>
> According to Jewish tradition, the commandments of Torah are considered to be divine rules of proper Jewish conduct bind-ing upon all who are a part of God's covenant established at Sinai . . . Observing Torah does not make the Jew righteous . . . Disobedience can result in the loss of the covenant relationship with God unless the Jew seeks forgiveness, relying upon God's covenantal faithfulness and mercy.[34]

If it is remembered that Paul is writing to Gentiles in Galatia, seeking to persuade them that they do not need to observe the whole Torah but that they already now are children of God, then it does not seem that there is any real difference between what Paul says and normative Jewish teaching. Both agree that the Jew's relationship with God is fundamentally dependent on the covenant and there-fore on faith. Paul, however, adds that now a similar relationship with God is available to Gentiles through faith in Jesus Christ. 'The only radical element in his preaching', says John Gager, is 'that Christ now offers to Gentiles what Israel always claimed to be possible only with the Torah . . . Not that the Torah ceases to be "use-ful" for Jews, but that its significance for Israel has now been repli-cated for Gentiles through Christ.'[35] Paul further argues that those Jews who deny this and insist that Gentiles have to be circumcised and become obedient to Torah have distorted the meaning of the

Law – making it, rather than the covenant, the basis for their relationship with God.

Paul returned to the same issue in his letter to the Romans. Jews, Paul insisted, could not claim superiority or a privileged relationship to God. Paul began by attacking Jewish 'boasting' – this was the claim that Jews had exclusive access to righteousness and the knowledge of God and that the only hope for Gentiles was to obey Torah.

Paul recognized that the Jews have been privileged to be entrusted with 'the very words of God' (Rom. 3.2). But he insisted that the Jews were no better than the Gentiles – 'Jews and Gentiles alike are all under sin' (Rom. 3.9). 'There is no difference, for all have sinned and fall short of the glory of God' (Rom. 3.23). 'Where then is boasting? It is excluded . . . Is God the God of Jews only? Is he not the God of Gentiles too? Yes, of Gentiles too, since there is only one God, who will justify the circumcised by faith and the uncircumcised through that same faith' (Rom. 3.27–30).

At once, Paul goes on to rebut the charge that he is nullifying the Law, claiming that he upholds the Law (Rom 3.31). In chapter 4, he argues, as he had done in Galatians, that God's covenant with Abraham, which preceded the Law, was based on faith. 'Abraham believed God, and it was credited to him as righteousness' (Rom. 4.3). The Law, which points the way of obedience to God, also makes people aware of their sin and their failure to observe it (Rom. 5.20). Paul, having ruled out a possible misunderstanding that we should go on sinning so that grace may increase, in chapter 7 returns to his point that the Law, which is spiritual, makes us aware of our disobedience and sin. Although this section is written in terms of 'I', it is probably intended, as has already been suggested, as a description of a universal human experience and is not primarily autobiographical.[36]

Paul's concern is to show that the Jew does not have a privileged status with God and to argue that all people are under sin and in need of the free justification by God through the redemption that came by Jesus Christ (Rom. 3.24). Paul emphasizes the role that the Law has in making a person, whether Jew or Gentile, aware of his or her sinfulness. He points to a new possibility for those who are in Christ who live 'in accordance with the Spirit' (Rom. 8.5). He does not, however, deny that the Law was given by God and implies that both the covenant with Abraham and the new covenant in Jesus Christ are both dependent on God's gracious promise to be appropriated by faith. Judaism and Christianity are, therefore, if we follow Paul, both to be seen as religions of covenant and grace. The Law, given by God, was the way in which Jews were called to respond to that gracious promise. Christians were called to respond by imitation of Jesus Christ, who in his total obedience to the Father, had fulfilled the Law (Rom. 5.19). Paul frequently appeals to the example of Christ as a pattern for human behaviour. For example, he urges the Philippians: 'Your attitude should be the same as that of Christ Jesus' (Phil. 2.5; cf. Col. 3.5–16; Eph. 5.1–2). In his letter to the Romans, his exposition of justification in Christ is followed by a call to his readers 'to offer your bodies as living sacrifices, holy and pleasing to God' (Rom. 12.1 – note the strong 'therefore' with which this section is introduced). Yet it is not suggested that such self-offering is an attempt to win God's favour. Rather it is a response to God's love shown in Jesus Christ – a way of life which should be characterized by 'love, joy, peace, patience, kindness, goodness, faithfulness, gentleness and self-control' (Gal. 5.22–23). The Law too, properly understood, is 'a delight', 'a lamp to my feet' and 'the joy of my heart' (Ps. 119.92, 105, 111).

For Paul, in Christ, God's gracious covenant with the people of Israel was now thrown open to all people. This was the long-awaited extension of the covenant made with Abraham, not a rejection of it. The 'mystery' or 'secret plan' of God revealed to Paul was, in the words of the epistle to the Ephesians, 'that through the gospel the Gentiles are heirs together with Israel, members of one body, and sharers together in the promise in Christ Jesus' (Eph. 3.6) – and, as Paul strenuously argued, Gentile membership of that one body did not require of them circumcision and obedience to the Law.

9

AN ENDURING COVENANT

Have Christians replaced the Jews as the people of God or should they regard Jews as still a people of God? If so are there two people of God and two parallel covenants or just the one covenant with Israel into which Gentiles have been admitted in Christ. Or should we recognize God's presence in all the great world religions?

I once asked in a pamphlet whether Paul thought of himself as a Jew or as a Christian – partly to make the point that it was not until some years after his death that the split between church and synagogue became complete. *The Times* briefly reported this and in response I received a letter from my mentor Lord Coggan, a former Archbishop of Canterbury and at that time Chair of the Council of Christians and Jews, pointing out Paul's frequent use of the phrase 'in Christ'. For example, 'if anyone is in Christ, he is a new creation; the old has gone, the new has come' (II Cor. 5.18). This new relationship with God was available to Jews as well as Gentiles. It is not enough to suggest that Paul's only concern was that Gentiles might come to know God through faith in Jesus Christ. To recognize Jesus as the Christ was also for a Jew to be transformed in his faith – perhaps because it implied that the promises of the end time were being fulfilled.

Yet, I do not think from this that one should conclude that Paul therefore wrote off the Jews' covenantal relationship with God. Francis Watson, using a sociological approach, distinguishes five clear stages in Paul's missionary activity. At an early stage of his Christian activity, Paul had preached the gospel only to Jews. He then began to preach to the Gentiles as a response to the failure of preaching among the Jews. Third, Paul and other Antiochene Jewish

Christians did not require full submission to the Law from their Gentile converts. Fourth, the abandonment of parts of the Law of Moses was intended to make it easier for Gentiles to become Christians; it helped to increase the success of Christian preaching. Finally, the Gentile mission thus involved the separation of the church from the synagogue.[1]

It does not follow, however, that because Paul concentrated on the conversion of the Gentiles, he had lost interest in preaching to the Jews. Paul himself in his letter to Romans said the gospel is the 'power of salvation, first for the Jew and then for the Gentile' – a phrase which mirrored Acts' account of the pattern of his preaching (Rom. 1.16; cf. Rom. 2.9–10; I Cor. 1.18–25). According to Acts, even in Rome Paul first speaks to the leaders of the Jews (Acts 28.17) as had been his custom throughout his missionary endeavours – although admittedly Francis Watson regards the Acts of the Apostles as historically unreliable.

Acts also shows Paul as observing purification rites. In Cenchrea, on his way to Jerusalem, he took a Nazirite vow (Acts 18.18). Once arrived in Jerusalem, James and the elders of the church told Paul of the accusation made against him that he was said to teach the Jews 'who live among the Gentiles to turn away from Moses, telling them not to circumcise their children or live according to our customs' (Acts 21.21). To rebut this charge, Paul agreed to the suggestion that he should join four men in purification rites at the Temple so that everybody would know 'that there is no truth in these reports about you, but that you yourself are living in obedience to the Law' (Acts 21.24).

Francis Watson also makes too sharp a division between Gentile and Jewish believers in Jesus. It was not until the second century that the church became so predominantly a Gentile body. The members of the church in Jerusalem, who were Jewish, continued to observe the Torah, although the situation began to change after the destruction of Jerusalem.

As to Paul's own practice, there is some uncertainty and he may have regarded himself as having a special dispensation because of his particular vocation. In I Corinthians 9.20–21, he wrote: 'To the Jews

I become like a Jew, to win the Jews. To those under the Law I became like one under the Law (though I myself am not under the Law). To those not having the Law, I became like one not having the Law (though I am not free from God's Law but am under Christ's Law).' Paul was clear that Gentiles did not have to observe the Law, but he tried to avoid giving offence to Jews. Writing to the Corinthians, Paul said: 'So whether you eat or drink or whatever you do, do it all for the glory of God. Do not cause anyone to stumble, whether Jews, Greeks or the church of God – even as I try to please everybody in every way. For I am not seeking my own good but the good of many, so that they may be saved' (I Cor. 10.31–33). The Jewish writer Alan Segal suggests that, like Daniel, Paul became a vegetarian, which 'for the most stringent Pharisee would eliminate the issues of acceptable slaughter of meat and idolatry'.[2] Certainly Paul wrote that 'if what I eat causes my brother to fall into sin, I will never eat meat again, so that I will not cause him to fall' (I Cor. 8.13).

Paul seems to have avoided giving unnecessary offence to observant Jews. There is also no evidence that Paul told Jewish believers in Jesus to abandon their observance of the Law.

The situation, however, changed quite quickly. By the end of the first century, in a predominantly Gentile church, not only were Jewish Christians not expected to keep the Law but Jewish observance itself came under attack.

Justin Martyr, in the second century, states that he would accept into Christian fellowship those Jews who continued to observe Torah, provided they did not seek to persuade Gentile Christians to follow the Mosaic Law. He admitted that others rejected the openness of his view. By the fourth century, the church had ruled that it was heretical even for believers of Jewish birth to keep the Law.[3]

Was the first covenant at an end?

Paul tried to hold together three deep-seated convictions: that in Christ there was a new creation; that the covenant had been opened to the Gentiles and third, his belief that God was faithful to the promise made to the Jewish people. The struggle involved may have resulted in some inconsistencies, as Heikki Räisänen has suggested. Räisänen found evidence that Paul believed that the Law both is and is not still valid and that Paul did not clearly differentiate between cultic requirements of the Torah and the moral Law.[4]

Some writers, continuing the traditional position of the church, insist that Paul thought that with the coming of Christ, the old covenant was at an end. E. P. Sanders, for example, in the concluding chapter of his *Paul and Palestinian Judaism*, writes: 'Paul in fact explicitly denies that the Jewish Covenant can be effective for salvation, thus consciously denying the basis of Judaism . . . More important, the Covenantal promises to Abraham do not apply to his descendants, but to Christians.'[5]

The British scholar N. T. Wright reaches a rather similar conclusion. Wright interprets the term 'Christ' in a collective sense. Paul, he says uses '"Christ" as a shorthand way of referring to that unity and completeness, and mutual participation, which belongs to the Church that is found "in Christ", that is, in fact, the people of the Messiah.'[6] In this new covenant community the distinction between Jew and Gentile is done away. '*All* those who believe in Jesus Christ and are baptized into him form one single family, so that there are not, in Christ, *different* families composed of Jews on the one hand and Gentiles, or Gentile Christians, on the other.'[7] 'For Paul,' Wright insists, 'there was only one way of salvation, namely, faith in Jesus Christ.'[8]

Wright recognizes that his views are in opposition to Stendahl and Gaston and others who speak of two covenants. Krister Stendahl, for example, writes with reference to Romans 9–11:

It should be noted that Paul does not say that when the time of God's kingdom, the consummation, comes Israel will accept Jesus as the Messiah. He says only that the time will come when 'all Israel will be saved' (11.26). It is stunning to note that Paul writes this whole section of Romans (10.18—11.36) without using the name of Jesus Christ. This includes the final doxology

(11.33–36), the only such doxology in his writings without any Christological element . . .

It is tempting to suggest that in important respects Paul's thought here approximates to an idea well documented in later Jewish thought from Maimonides to Franz Rosenzweig. Christianity – and in the case of Maimonides, also Islam – is seen as the conduit of Torah, for the declaration of both monotheism and the moral order to the Gentiles. The differences are obvious, but the similarity should not be missed: Paul's reference to God's mysterious plan is an affirmation of a God-willed coexistence between Judaism and Christianity in which the missionary urge to convert Israel is held in check.[9]

I find it helpful to compare Paul's view of the majority of Jews with that of the elder son in the parable of the Prodigal Son. The father welcomes the return of the prodigal son and holds a party for him. The elder son refuses to join the celebrations. The father goes out and pleads with him, saying, 'My son, you are always with me, and everything I have is yours.' We are not told whether the elder son agreed to join the party. Whether or not he did so, he remained the son – none of his rights and privileges were taken away. Few of Paul's Jewish contemporaries shared his experience of new life in Jesus nor his conviction that God had acted to open the covenant to the Gentiles, but that does not imply that their existing status with God was changed. It was not a matter of removing existing privileges, but of extending them to others. In a similar way, those Christians today who, despite strong criticism from some fellow-Christians, recognize God's presence in other faith communities, are not thereby denying God's continuing presence in the Christian church. Paul longed for his fellow-Jews to enjoy with him the new life in the Spirit. He spoke of their blindness and disobedience, but he did not suggest that they had been disinherited.

Romans 9–11

Paul begins his major discussion of the relation of the Jews and Gentile believers in Jesus by speaking of his 'great grief and unceasing sorrow' (Rom. 9.2 NEB). The majority of Jews did not appreciate that the 'mystery' made known to Paul – that in Christ the covenant had been opened to the Gentiles. This caused him great distress. It was also the reason why he suffered bitter and sometimes violent opposition from some Jewish opponents (II Cor. 11.23–29; cf. Acts), as well as criticism from some Jewish believers in Jesus.

Having spoken of his anguish, Paul affirms the special and continuing heritage of the Jewish people. 'Theirs is the adoption as sons; theirs the divine glory, the covenants, the receiving of the Law, the temple worship and the promises. Theirs are the patriarchs and from them is traced the human ancestry of Christ, who is over all. God be for ever praised!' (Rom. 9.4–5 NIV alternative reading). Paul then says that God's word has not in fact failed because, as so often in the history of Israel, a minority, or remnant, of whom Paul was one, has believed God's message. There is then some speculation on why God chooses one person and not another as, for example, in the case of the brothers Esau and Jacob.

Paul then ponders Israel's unbelief. Their failure to accept the gospel was because they pursued righteousness 'not by faith but as if it were by works' (Rom. 9.32). 'They sought to establish their own [righteousness] and did not submit to God's righteousness' (Rom. 10.3). Paul recognizes a blindness by the majority of Jews but denies that their fall was irreversible (Rom. 11.11). Rather it was intended by God to open the way to salvation for the Gentiles, who had no reason to boast against the Jews, just as earlier Paul had said that the Jews had no reason for boasting. God's favour is in all cases a matter of grace.

In any case, God's ultimate purpose remains the salvation of Israel. As Paul writes:

Israel has experienced a hardening in part until the full number of the Gentiles has come in. And so all Israel will be saved . . . As far as the gospel is concerned, they are enemies on your account; but as far as election is concerned, they are loved on account of the patriarchs, for God's gifts and his call are irrevocable (Rom. 11.26, 28).

Both Gentiles and Jews have been disobedient to God but thereby have discovered God's mercy (Rom. 11.32).

Paul, therefore, seems to affirm both that God's gifts and the call to Israel are eternal and that most Jews are blind because they have put obedience to the Law in the place of God's new call for faith in Christ. A fundamental component of Israel's self-understanding, the privileged relation to God provided by the Mosaic covenant, has been permanently revoked. Yet Paul goes to great lengths to deny certain inferences that were already being drawn in his own time and which have served as the traditional view of Paul. At three points in chapter 11 he denies that Israel has been rejected by God. In 11.2 he states simply that God has not rejected the people whom he foreknew. In 11.11 he denies that their stumbling leads to their fall. 'By no means!' is his reply. Then in 11.28, he affirms that 'the gifts and the call of God are irrevocable'. Paul longed for the day when many other Jews would share his understanding of God's purposes and yet when he says that 'all Israel will be saved', he does not say that all Israel will come to faith in Christ. Paul also has the humility, not so evident among all scholars, to say that no one has known 'the mind of the Lord' (Rom. 11.34).

Is Paul's teaching, however, a warrant for efforts to convert Jews to Christianity or is it God's purpose that the majority of Jewish people should continue to witness to God by their faithful obedience to the Torah?

Jewish attitudes

This is a matter of heated debate. A major stumbling block to better Jewish–Christian relations is the missionary attempt by some Christians to convert Jews. Jews have a deep fear of Christian missionary activity. For many Jews such activity evokes memories of forced conversions and persecution.

Chief Rabbi Jonathan Sacks has written: 'The fact that the great universal monotheisms have not yet formally endorsed a plural world is the still unexorcised darkness at the heart of our religious situation.'[10]

Some Jews regard Christian missionary activity as even worse than the devastation of European Jewry by Adolf Hitler. Hitler destroyed the physical expression of Judaism, whereas Christian missionaries, if successful, would destroy the spiritual life of Judaism.[11]

Jews now see their calling to be, by example, 'a light to the Gentiles'. In contemporary Jewish writing there is frequent reference to God's covenant with all people through the covenant with Noah (Gen. 12.9 ff.). God's covenant with Israel is not exclusive in the sense that God is not concerned for Gentiles. Most Jews accept a pluralist position and affirm that the righteous of all nations will have a share in the world to come.[12]

Traditionally, if a Jew converted to another religion or married a non-Jew, the family would treat the person as dead and sit *shi'va*, that is to say go through the rites of mourning. In Edwina Currie's novel *She's Leaving Home*, Mannheim says: 'In the old days in the *shtetl* when a son or a daughter married out the father would hold a funeral service. For a girl especially, because she takes with her the ability to bear Jewish children. They would offer prayers for the dead as she walked away.' Maurice replies: 'You can't cold shoulder your own kith and kin.'[13] Except among the ultra-orthodox, few Jews today question the right of individuals freely to change from one religion to another, but 'marrying out' is very often a cause of tension and there is strong Jewish dislike of organized Christian missionary activity.

Jews resent the active and well-financed missionary groups, often based in the USA, which harass or 'target' some of the Jewish community. Their methods are felt to be dishonest and aggressive. The Jewish community has an understandable insecurity, not just because of the past, but because in most European countries Jews are a small minority. Further, for demographic reasons and because of 'marrying out', most European Jewish communities are decreasing.

Although the decline is not because there are many conversions to Christianity, there are some and these are often highly publicized. In the USA, the position is rather different, as the Jewish community is larger and it is a society used to vigorous religious competition.

A particular difficulty is caused by 'Messianic Jews'. These are people who are Jewish by birth but who believe that 'Yeshua' is the Messiah. Not all Christians of Jewish birth are Messianic Jews. Some are active members of main-stream churches.[14] Messianic Jews usually wish to preserve some Jewish practices, perhaps keeping Saturday as the day of rest or using Hebrew in worship, and claim to be Jews. The Jewish community does not regard anyone who believes that Jesus is Lord to be a Jew. There is a dispute, therefore, about what it means to be a Jew and an understandable Jewish sensitivity to any suggestion that Jewishness is a racial characteristic. Some Messianic Jews, especially those called 'Jews for Jesus', have been particularly active in efforts to convert Jews. 'Jews for Jesus' have received support from some Christians, but many church leaders have distanced themselves from such activities, which undermine the fragile new relationships which are based on dialogue.

Christian attitudes

Until Christians clearly repudiate conversionist activity aimed at Jews, there will be an uneasiness in the relationship. Christians are deeply divided on whether or not they should attempt to convert Jews. A wide range of views was recognized at the 1988 Lambeth Conference of Anglican bishops. The document *Jews, Christians and Muslims: The Way of Dialogue* acknowledges that:

> At one pole, there are those Christians whose prayer is that Jews, without giving up their Jewishness, will find their fulfilment in Jesus the Messiah. Indeed some regard it as their particular vocation and responsibility to share their faith with Jews ... Other Christians, however, believe that in fulfilling the Law and the prophets, Jesus validated the Jewish relationship with God, whilst

opening up this way for Gentiles through his own person. For others, the Holocaust has changed their perception, so that until Christian lives bear a truer witness, they feel a divine obligation to affirm the Jews in their worship and sense of the God and Father of Jesus.[15]

Some Christians feel that mission is integral to the gospel. Indeed not to evangelize Jews is regarded by some Christians as itself anti-Semitic. In his *Hated Without a Cause?*, Graham Keith writes:

> Today the claim is often made that any attempt to evangelize Jews is an act of anti-Semitism. Paul is a standing witness against this both in his attitudes and in his practice. Indeed, he would turn the tables on these critics of Jewish evangelism. His own stance would suggest that to withhold the gospel from the Jews – whether because it is thought that rabbinic Judaism is an adequate alternative to Christianity or because Jews are considered so hardened that it is impossible for them to be converted – is itself a form of anti-Semitism.

In a footnote, Keith quotes the words of a contemporary Jewish Christian that 'any effort on the part of Christians to exclude Jews from their evangelism is – however well intentioned – a form of spiritual anti-Semitism'.[16]

Other Christians who are uneasy with missions aimed at converting Jews have tried to reinterpret the meaning of the word 'mission'. Sometimes there is talk of a shared mission of those who believe in God to an unbelieving world. Others distinguish between mission or 'proselytism' and 'witness'. 'Proselytism' or 'mission' are used in a pejorative sense of the organized attempt to win members of one faith over to another and to get them to change their religion. 'Witness', by contrast, is used of a telling of what the Christian believes God has done in Jesus Christ. It is a sharing of experience, which includes listening to the spiritual experience of the other. No attempt is made to pressurize the other and it is stressed that the response is a matter between the individual and God.[17]

'God's covenant with the Jews has never been recalled'

Redefining mission may be a useful internal ploy, but a new partnership of Jews and Christians requires nothing less than a glad recognition that the Jews remain a 'people of God'. Indeed the church needs to make a similar acknowledgment of God's presence in every faith community.

The claim that God's covenant with Israel is still valid is becoming a commonplace of church statements on Christian–Jewish relations, although these statements are too little known or acted upon. How the covenants are related remains a matter of debate.[18]

The view that God has rejected his covenant with Israel is now, however, seen to be wrong for several reasons:

1. It calls in question God's trustworthiness and faithfulness to his promises.
2. It ignores the continuing spiritual fecundity of Israel and the faithfulness of the Jewish people.
3. It is based on a misreading of Jesus' attitude to the Torah.
4. It may also be a misunderstanding of the teaching of Paul.

God's covenant with Israel is eternal, because it is based on God's gracious choice of his people and his rescuing of them from the land of Egypt. A response is called for, but God's promise is not conditional. Otherwise, as Paul van Buren asked:

> If God is not faithful to His people, if He does not stand by His Covenant with Israel, why should we think that He will be any more faithful to His Gentile Church?[19]

Further, throughout the centuries, many Jews have remained faithful to the covenant and obedient to Torah. Their faithfulness witnesses to the continuing validity of the covenant.

Paul, it seems, did hope that other Jews would come to share his conviction about Jesus Christ. Yet in the letter to the Romans, by which time he must have come to recognize that only a few Jews would accept the gospel, he acknowledged that Israel's unbelief was also part of God's purpose. Maybe this can help us to see that God seeks different responses of different faith communities. We should not assume that God has only one way of dealing with humanity. As Rabbi Irving Greenberg has said, 'the God who chose once, can choose and choose again'.[20] We are back to the challenge of Shaye J. D. Cohen that we have to give theological legitimacy to the other.[21]

The other is not only the Jewish people, but Hindus, Muslims, Buddhists, Sikhs, indigenous people and many more. It is not enough just to recognize that Jews, like Christians, are a people of God. We need to move to a consistent universalism, which recognizes God's presence in every faith community. This, as Rosemary Ruether, has written,

> would solve the dilemma of Christian competitive negation of Judaism, and other religions, by moving to a consistent universalism which would allow every human culture, and its quest for truth and justice, to have its own validity. God as the centre of creation and redemption is not manifest through only one centre, through one people and one land, but as the centre for all peoples and all lands, defined in distinct and different ways . . .[22]

Rosemary Radford Ruether goes on to make a passionate plea for mutual respect and co-operation:

> In order to live in peace and justice on the planet, the different human cultures and religions need to find concrete ways of affirming their mutual respect for one another. There also must be some working consensus on what justice and human rights mean as the basis for an international rule of Law by which all people must be judged in their treatment of others, both within and between their national communities.[23]

It is the suffering of humanity that demands an end to religious exclusivism so that the spiritual resources of the great religions are released to encourage co-operation and the healing of the nations. Already in some of the great inter-religious gatherings that marked the last year of the twentieth century, and the growing emphasis on the values that are shared by the great faiths, we see the path ahead, but the same year was marked by ethnic cleansing in Kosovo. There is a constant need to ensure that the progress made is understood and secured while together we tackle outstanding issues and co-operate in the healing of the world.

10

THE PATH AHEAD

In this book, I have concentrated on outlining the theological re-thinking required of Christians, if they are to give thanks to God that the Jews are still here.

But this is only a preliminary to journeying forward with Jews and other people of faith in service of the world. For 'Jewish–Christian dialogue may have a number of objectives but its ultimate aim is to contribute towards a better world – a world in which the will of God is done; a world of justice and peace.'[1]

When the Council of Christians and Jews was formed in 1942 one of its objectives was to bear witness to the ethical values that Judaism and Christianity held in common. From the early days of Christian–Jewish dialogue there has been a desire to speak together on moral matters and to act together to combat prejudice and discrimination. Christians and Jews have talked together, for example, about the values of family life. They have campaigned together for religious freedom in the former Soviet Union.

Even so, recognizing the measure of friendship that has grown up between individual Jews and Christians and their co-operation on many social and moral issues, the period since the Second World War has been dominated by the need to remove inherited misunderstanding and suspicion between Jews and Christians.

Several people are suggesting that now is the time to move forward to affirm the moral values which are shared by the two faith communities.

At a service to mark the fiftieth anniversary of the Council of Christians and Jews, Lord Coggan, a former Archbishop of Canterbury, said:

There is a very real danger that we may rest content with dialogue and fail to push on from it to the next stage of our journey together . . . We must advance from dialogue to a sense of joint-trusteeship. At the heart of the Jewish faith and of the Christian faith is the conviction that Jews and Christians alike have been recipients of divine truths which are of immense importance.

Lord Coggan went on to enumerate some of these, such as the belief in a God who cares for each individual and for the creation; a recognition that the body is a temple for God's abiding; the necessity of a break from the routine of work by observing 'the Sabbath'.[2]

Similarly, Professor Ewert Cousins of Fordham University has written recently that in concert with other religions, Christianity and Judaism should put 'their energies into solving the common human problems that threaten our future on the earth . . . Just to meet, even creatively, on the spiritual level is not enough. They must channel their spiritual resources towards the solution of global problems.'[3]

Attempts to do this are being made. The International Council of Christians and Jews issued a useful statement which highlights the particular view of humanity, the world and God, which the two religions share. The common belief that the world is the creation of the One God means that the world is given into the care and stewardship of humanity, which is called to serve and protect it. It means also that each human being is created in the image of God and therefore is infinitely precious to God and that human beings are responsible for each other.[4]

Such a document leaves certain questions unanswered. For example, how are these 'generalities' to be translated into more specific agreement? There is sharp difference of opinion on many matters within each community. For example, on birth control, homosexuality, divorce or the place of women.

Attempts, however, are being made to address these more particular concerns. Early in 1994 an international Jewish–Christian conference in Jerusalem discussed Genetic Engineering, Ethnicity, Multi-Culturalism and Integration, Religious Education in Pluralistic Societies, The Search for Spirituality in the Modern World, Autonomy and Authority, The Quality and Quantity of Life, The Beginnings of Life. Papers included ones on Ageing and Ageism and the Judaic Perspective on Handicap.

Jews and Christians are also meeting to talk about feminist issues or ecology. To hope that a Jewish–Christian consensus or position can be reached on these subjects may be an illusion. Instead, perhaps, such gatherings indicate that the discussion of ethical and social matters is becoming both inter-religious and inter-disciplinary.

Another question is whether there is a specifically Jewish–Christian witness? In the USA 'interfaith' was sometimes used to refer to the well-established co-operation of Roman Catholics, Protestants and Jews. Now, Muslims are increasingly being involved in the conversation. The National Conference of Christians and Jews (NCCJ) has welcomed Muslims as members and changed its name to the National Conference. In 1998 at the highly evocative site of Auschwitz, Jews, Christians and Muslims met to discuss 'Religion and Violence: Religion and Peace'.[5] In Britain, where the Council of Christians and Jews is still very active a Three Faiths Forum for Jews, Christians and Muslims has been founded, although some members of other religions would rightly object if Jews, Christians and Muslims spoke, as occasionally happens, of their religions as 'The Three Monotheistic Faiths'.

Indeed, Christians, Jews and Muslims are increasingly sharing in wider and very varied interfaith activity. The growing desire that religions should work together for peace and to uphold the moral values that they share was shown, for example, in the 'Declaration Toward a Global Ethic', adopted at the Parliament of the World's Religions in Chicago in 1993. The 1999 Parliament, in Cape Town, followed this up with a 'Call to the Guiding Institutions', which attempts to engage people of many disciplines with people of all faiths in grappling with the problems facing the human community.[6] In August 2000, one thousand religious and spiritual leaders from around the world met, for the first time, in the General Assembly hall of the United Nations and signed a Commitment to

Global Peace in which they pledged 'to work together to promote the inner and outer conditions that foster peace and the non-violent management and resolution of conflict'. They appealed to the followers of all religious traditions and to the human community as a whole, 'to co-operate in building peaceful societies, to seek mutual understanding through dialogue where there are differences, to refrain from violence, to practice compassion, and to uphold the dignity of all life.'[7]

Despite these optimistic signs, prejudice, violence and bitter ethnic hostility, as well as poverty, still seems endemic. Yet if members of the world religions can put behind them centuries of hostility, they may be able to help other people move forward from inherited conflict. As the dark clouds that threaten the world lift for a moment we may catch a glimpse of another mountain peak ahead. It is the mountain that the prophet Micah saw long ago. It is the mountain of the Lord 'where nations will hammer their swords into ploughs and their spears into pruning knives . . . and where everyone will live in peace . . . and no one will be afraid' (Micah 4.1–4).

RESPONSE

Rabbi Tony Bayfield

Chief Executive, Reform Synagogues of Great Britain

There is a joke that gets recycled on a fairly regular basis. It goes along the following lines.

> Question: What are the four proofs that Jesus was Jewish?
> Answer: (1) He lived at home until he was 30.
>   (2) He went into the family business.
>   (3) He thought his mother was a virgin.
>   (4) She thought he was God.

On one level, the joke can be viewed as an example of that self-deprecating Jewish humour which has become universally familiar in recent decades. It relies on the supposedly intense, even neurotic, relationship that Jewish men have with their parents, particularly their mothers. There are hints of Philip Roth's Portnoy: 'A Jewish man with parents alive is a fifteen year old boy and will remain a fifteen year old boy until they die!'[1] But on another level, the joke clearly reveals a widespread Jewish scepticism. If the virgin birth is highly unlikely, the concept of incarnation is simply a joke. A joke that shows no signs of losing its popularity. In that lies much of the imbalance, the lack of proportionality that characterizes where Jewish–Christian dialogue has reached as we enter the third Christian millennium. Marcus Braybrooke suggests, for a number of cogent reasons, that dialogue has attained something of a plateau. The failure by most Jews to take Christian theology seriously may offer an additional reason.

Braybrooke is a man of quite remarkable insight and sensitivity. In this clear and tolerant book, he has explained to Christians what is required of them if they are to put Christian–Jewish relations on the kind of level that would take Judaism seriously, grant unqualified respect, make true partnership possible and eliminate fear, anger and resentment. This is a brave agenda, bravely and successfully accomplished. What Braybrooke does not do is to suggest to the Jewish world what it needs to do to achieve a certain measure of balance, symmetry, reciprocity. That, I would guess, is my task.

By and large, Jews have gone into dialogue with Christians with a wholly understandable and deeply felt shopping list. It goes something like this:

'First, we would like a full and unequivocal apology for anti-Judaism and anti-Semitism. We see much that is anti-Jewish in the New Testament and much that is anti-Semitic in Christian writings and behaviour from the patristic period through to the end of the Dark Ages; from the Crusades, Inquisition and anti-Jewish legislation of the Middle Ages to the pogroms of late nineteenth-century Eastern Europe. We see clear connections with Nazi anti-Semitism, the greatest catastrophe of two thousand years of largely miserable encounter with Christian civilization. We want the fullest, deepest acknowledgment. We want an extended and unequivocal period of unreserved apology. We need to know that you really, really acknowledge your guilt and repent.

Second, we want Christians to deal effectively with the anti-Judaism that is embedded in your teaching and preaching, in your stained glass and statuary, in the very gospel text itself. We are very disturbed that you carry on solemnly reading aloud from texts such as 'ye are of your father the devil, and the lusts of your father ye will do. He was a murderer from the beginning and abode not in the truth, because there is no truth in him'.[2] As if it were gospel! When are you going to tackle your perpetuation of anti-Jewish propaganda? You simply have to address in full the decidedly unflattering portrait that the New Testament paints of the Pharisees. After all, twentieth-century Jews are the direct descendants of rabbinic Judaism, of pharisaic Judaism – as the title of Rabbi Lionel

Blue's first and finest book *To Heaven with Scribes and Pharisees* implies.'[3]

The first two items on the Jewish shopping list are acknowledgment and rectification. But the list goes on:

'We are fed up to the teeth with Christian triumphalism and imperialism. We are not prepared to hear any more that the covenant with the synagogue and with the Jewish people has been broken. We need to know that you acknowledge that ours is a valid, independent faith, a living tradition, a source of revelation and just as good a religion as Christianity. We are not prepared to be treated as forsaken or rejected. Enough of this *Old* Testament slight. We are sick to death of listening to "Thought for the Day" on Radio 4, and hearing that Jesus came to fulfil Judaism, to complete it, to take it to new heights and then to be treated to interminable homilies about the Pharisees being vanquished six-love, six-love in argument. Enough of "Judaism, religion of law, nasty boo hiss" and "Christianity, religion of love, hip hip hooray". After all, when Jesus taught the central importance of loving one another, he was only quoting Leviticus 19.18.'

And on:

'Don't think, moreover, that you can get away with suggesting that we are, in much of our behaviour, really Christians, it is just that we don't realize it. Saving our souls by dubbing us "anonymous Christians" is condescending and imperialistic at the same time. We are Jews and proud of it and that has to be good enough in itself.

Of course, much of the trouble centres on the accusation of deicide. That needs eliminating once and for all. Leave aside whether Jesus was God or not, to label all Jews as murderers is preposterous and, anyway, crucifixion was a Roman rather than a Jewish form of punishment.

Last, but by no means least, it follows that you Christians need, once and for all, to renounce your claims on Jewish souls. We Jews are few in number – less than 14 million of us the world over. We worry ourselves sick about Jewish numbers and Jewish survival. The last thing that we need is to add to those worries through fear of Christian missionary activities so often aimed at our most vulnerable adherents. There *is* salvation outside the church. Kindly lay off and state unequivocally and once and for all that you do not need or want Jews to convert to Christianity.'

That sums up the shopping list – apologize, confess and eradicate your anti-Judaism and anti-Semitism. Exonerate us of our alleged crimes. Abandon your designs on our souls and allow us to be what Freiderich Heer called us, namely, 'God's First Love',[4] a love that has never been withdrawn.

In short, please leave us alone.

I hope that I have conveyed in my tone something of the anger, hurt, anxiety, suspicion and fear that is still much more present than might be supposed.

For completeness, let me just add that to this 'religious' shopping list have been appended a number of 'political' demands which flow with emotional as much as philosophical logic.

'Stop knocking the state of Israel, stop siding with the Palestinians, stop trying to Christianize the death camps of the Shoah with convents and crosses, stop beatifying Jewish converts to Christianity and let's have an honest appraisal of Pope Pius XII.'

The shopping list is, let me repeat, a very understandable one and I do not wish to denigrate it by characterizing it as a shopping list. However, it has very strong overtones of 'this is what we want from you – your behaviour over the last two thousand years makes it our entitlement'. It also has very strong overtones of Jewish self-defence – attempting to eradicate those teachings and attitudes which have led to so much suffering and pain in the past.

With clarity and sensitivity, Braybrooke has not only acknowledged the shopping list – while never demeaning it with such a title – but goes to great lengths to acknowledge its validity and to show that it can be met in full without irreparably damaging Christianity or compromising core faith commitments (as opposed to credal formulations).

Braybrooke stresses the fact that Jesus was a Jew. He lived at a time of great intellectual and religious ferment and stands fully in the context of passionate discussion about the will of God which characterizes the period. He had a deep sense that the kingdom was at hand but that was not out of the Jewish ordinary for the times. Uncovering the historical Jesus is an extremely difficult task to accomplish by virtue of the way the New Testament came to be written, but it simply is not necessary to see Jesus as completely at odds with the Pharisees. It is clear that Jesus was put to death by the Romans and if there may well have been a degree of complicity shown by some of the Jewish leadership, it is clear that *what* killed Jesus was Roman imperialism, not the Jewish people down the ages.

Braybrooke is clear that the 'partings of the ways'[5] came about as a result of Christianity pushing the Jewish tradition towards the universalist end of the spectrum – no circumcision for Gentile converts – while rabbinic Judaism opted for a higher degree of particularism. There is no particular value judgment in either choice. He even explains resurrection and incarnation in ways which Jews cannot only begin to understand but find echoes in subsequent Jewish tradition and see as powerful religious insights. Incarnation and resurrection will always remain part of someone else's religious story for Jews, but Braybrooke expounds both in a way that stops us patronizing or joking. He demands an end to all religious exclusivism and sees the path ahead in similar terms to Hans Küng[6] – as an ending of the war between religions and the building of a partnership, based on mutual respect for the good of humanity and the globe. The covenant with the Jews has not been broken; Christianity is not the only way; there is much to be learnt from each other and achieved through co-operation.

What is remarkable about Braybrooke's position is not just its openness, sensitivity and generosity. It is not just that he has heard the Jewish list and responded fully, clearly, intelligently and in a manner that feels faithful and authentic to both traditions. What is also remarkable is that there isn't even a hint of annoyance or irritability. Given that he has worked with Jews and in the field of Christian–Jewish dialogue for many years, the absence of irritation with a small, vocal, neurotic minority is truly remarkable. After all, we Jews are survivors, and however much survivors deserve compassion and understanding, they are seldom the easiest group to deal with.

Interestingly, that doyen of Catholic-Jewish dialogue in the United States, Eugene Fisher, recently gave a lecture which reflected a level of frustration and irritation that is altogether understandable.[7] Fisher argued that the Catholic Church had made truly outstanding progress in recognition and rectification in the final third of the twentieth century. It had really opened itself to dialogue. Yet this very contact and openness had exposed the Catholic 'elephant' to all sorts of criticism from the Jewish 'mouse' – political criticisms over whom the church should declare saints, criticisms of the papacy, particularly of Pope Pius XII. It had also brought a very Jewish but un-Catholic irreverence to discussion of Vatican texts and Jewish spokespersons still seemed unsatisfied with the considerable humility shown by the church in acknowledging its responsibilities for medieval anti-Judaism (not quite the same as the anti-Semitism of the Nazis).

In a response to Fisher's lecture,[8] I suggested that the irritation was very understandable though some of the particular 'targets' were misconceived. What Fisher was actually saying, I felt, was that just because the Catholic elephant is infinitely larger than the Jewish mouse doesn't mean that it cannot feel vulnerable. That it needs to be left some self-respect, some sense of the magnificent truth of Christianity, some sense that its record of dealing with Jews does not completely undermine its claim to be a great faith tradition in the service of God and humanity. Perhaps I should add that, despite its truly welcome apologies, the Catholic Church has not yet fully addressed some of its teachings which continue to trouble Jews and marginalize Judaism.

Braybrooke gives a number of reasons as to why Christian–Jewish dialogue has reached something of a plateau – a reluctance shown by the churches to engage in that necessary theological rethinking, more pressing problems on both sides, divisions within both the Jewish and Christian worlds being three such reasons.

Fisher explains the plateau in other terms as well, by articulating his annoyance and irritation.

If we combine Braybrooke's generously one-sided explanation with what lies behind Fisher's irritation, something becomes absolutely crystal clear. If Jewish–Christian dialogue is to go significantly further, then there are some searching questions that need to be asked not just of the churches, but of the Jewish community as well. Since Braybrooke is too nice to ask those questions, I will now make that my task.

There is something about the Jewish shopping list which is significant. Find us innocent of deicide, get round the nasty bits in your scriptures, repent your anti-Semitism and leave us to be the people of God whom we have always been – is a remarkably untheological list of demands. Or, rather, it makes no demands on Jewish theology and implies that the issues for Christian theology are really 'your problem'. It doesn't 'engage' or 'connect' or seek to understand or clarify. That is not very surprising, since there is a significant Jewish tradition of not willingly engaging in theological dialogue. I say 'willingly' because it was something forced on Jews by the medieval disputations. However, if we move to the twentieth century, we find perhaps the two key intellectual figures of twentieth-century Orthodox Judaism taking a very strong line against dialogue.

The first is Eliezer Berkovits who writes: 'We are not as yet ready to enter into a fraternal dialogue with a church, a religion, that has been responsible for so much suffering, and which is ultimately responsible for the murder of our fathers and mothers, brothers and sisters in the present generation.'[9]

Berkovits' elucidator, Jonathan Sacks continues:

> Theologically, dialogue is pointless. Judaism is self-sufficient and does not need to consult Christianity to understand itself. Philosophically, a specific Jewish–Christian conversation has no special significance. Jews are open to ideas from other cultures; each is to be judged on its own merits; but there is no unique relationship between Judaism and Christianity . . . In particular, the concept of a common Judeo-Christian heritage has no meaning within Jewish frames of reference . . . what motivates Christians to dialogue has no counterpart in Judaism . . . dialogue would be frankly unethical.

What comes through in this summary by Jonathan Sacks of Berkovits' position is the pain and anger of Orthodox Judaism's most profound Holocaust theologian. However, it is pain and anger that has restrained many from any engagement in true dialogue. It is reinforced by the dominant figure of twentieth-century Orthodox Judaism, Rabbi J. B. Soloveitchik in an essay which appeared under the title 'Confrontation' in the American journal *Tradition* in 1964. Soloveitchik was explicit that the meeting or 'confrontation' between Jews and Christians should not take place at the theological level at all: 'our common interests lie not in the realm of faith, but in that of the secular orders'.[10] Soloveitchik argued that Jews and Christians could and should work together on such causes as social justice, but Judaism should not be willing or able to revise any of its historic stances in the pursuit of mutuality and reconciliation.[11]

While Orthodox Jewish leaders both in this country and abroad have, in many instances, gone far in associating themselves with Christian leaders, making common cause on moral and social issues, giving leadership to Councils devoted to Christian–Jewish understanding, dialogue in the sense of seeking to understand the beliefs and teachings of the other and in the sense of trying to make respectful theological space for the other has been left almost exclusively to Reform and Liberal Jews. The nearest parallel that I can think of is the lack of engagement up to this point by the Orthodox churches in the same process. The last thing that I would want to do is to minimize or qualify the importance of the contribution made by Reform and Liberal rabbis to Christian–Jewish dialogue. However, it is important to realize that not all of the Jewish world is 'in the same place' when it comes to this, or many other, subjects. But then Marcus Braybrooke, in his sensitivity, liberality and openness, in his call for rethinking doctrine, is also a radical and a pioneer and needs to be recognized as such.

Not being willing to revise historic stances is clearly an issue for some Jews and some Christians alike, but it has real implications for dialogue and for moving on from the present plateau. Let me introduce a personal note at this point. Marcus Braybrooke and I have shared dialogue groups for a decade and a half. What I can testify to – 'admit' – is that I have been changed immeasurably by the process. It hasn't weakened my fidelity to Judaism but it has certainly made me question and think through my faith and beliefs as in no other context. To borrow a rather naïve and simplistic metaphor, being taken on a guided tour of the Christian garden by sensitive and enlightened gardeners has enabled me to go back to my own garden and appreciate it in a new way, see weeds that I would never other- wise have recognized and understand that, however lovely and how- ever loved, mine is just one garden.

Real dialogue pushes Jews into addressing some of the issues that we have hitherto only been insisting that Christians address.

Dialogue forces Jews to recognize the extent to which many Christians are people of deep and intelligent faith; that the New Testament, however it is read, plays much the same role in Christian life as the Torah, the Five Books of Moses, plays in Judaism; that Christianity is a faith tradition whose adherents and teachings demand to be taken very seriously. By and large, in recent decades, Christians have been more able to take Judaism seriously than Jews Christianity. Remember the 'joke' with which I began this con- cluding chapter.

I now want to ask – of myself, of the Jewish world – a series of questions. The first is, are we prepared to take Jesus seriously?

For a whole host of reasons, few Jews have been able to approach the figure of Jesus with any kind of serious yet open mind, in – and I know this is an imperfect analogy – the way that we would approach Muhammad or Buddha. I do not want to go back into the history of the last two thousand years but, on some level, Jesus is associated with polemic, forced conversion, accusations of deicide as well as a theological doctrine which is particularly challenging for Jews. As a result, there is a widespread tendency for Jews, either consciously or unconsciously defensive and dismissive, to dismiss Jesus as a com- pletely unremarkable figure. Although understandable, it is, in a sense, remarkable given the Jewish tendency not to be backward when it comes to claiming famous figures with a Jewish background – take Marx and Freud, for example. To be sure, a number of Jewish scholars, Geza Vermes, Hyam Maccoby for example, have joined the quest for the historical Jesus, but I know that I am on safe ground in saying that they are atypical. The task is not made easier by the extreme difficulty of identifying the historical Jesus and separating him from the projections of many generations of faithful believers. John Bowden's insightful book *Jesus: The Unanswered Questions*[12] contains a painfully honest acknowledgment of this fact.

Nevertheless, the usually unarticulated dismissal of Jesus as a Galilean carpenter of little originality is far from helpful. Yes, Jesus lived at a time of apocalyptic speculation. Yes, Jesus lived at a time of messianic expectation. Yes, other Jews were also hailed as Messiah too. But that does not begin to explain how this particular Galilean carpenter became the focus of, I hope it is not offensive to phrase it in this way, the most successful religion the world has ever known. If Jews are really to acquire some sympathy for Christianity, some understanding, some fellow-feeling as opposed to presenting a list of justifiable demands, in other words if Jews are to take dialogue seriously, they are going to have to take the figure of Jesus, and not just Paul, seriously. If Christians need fully to accept Jesus as a Jew, Jews need fully to accept Jesus as a remarkable Jew. Are we prepared both to reclaim a famous son and also to try to understand what was so important about him?

A number of Jews have engaged on a serious scholarly level with the New Testament text. It will be clear from many of Marcus Braybrooke's comments that the text presents a range of problems to Jews.

First of all and as I have already indicated, as heirs to rabbinic Judaism and descendants of the scribes and Pharisees we don't appear in a very good light. We seem consistently to take an obtuse, insensitive, legalistic line as Pharisees over against the sensitivity and compassion of Jesus. When a man is in trouble, we walk past on the other side of the street. We appear to have a substantial responsibility for the crucifixion of Jesus. We appear blind to his enduring message of love and his bias towards the poor, needy and oppressed. We are possessive of our Judaism and reluctant to share it with Gentiles. We are everything that stands in the way of true humanity and true faith. The portrait is not a flattering one and allegorizing the Jew as every man is not much of a consolation.

Second, there are puzzles within the New Testament text, instances in which Jesus advances a position that was actually the position adopted by the rabbis, by Jewish Law, whereas the quoted Pharisaic position finds no parallels in contemporary Jewish literature.

Third, there are many occasions where Jesus is clearly teaching the Hebrew Bible or voicing views and using parables or *m'shalim*, images which find their parallel in rabbinic literature – but for which 'Judaism' appears to get no credit.

There is a considerable interest, therefore, among Jewish scholars and, dare I say, Jewish polemicists in taking the New Testament text and attempting to show that the Gospels, as well as being written after the events that they portray, have a strong element of 'party political manifesto' about them. I never fail to be moved by the courage and humility of scholars like Marcus Braybrooke in acknowledging the difficulties and complexities of a text that is so precious to Christianity. It moves me to ask three further questions.

First, how open are Jews to the really tough questions about the Hebrew Bible and the doctrines that have been erected on the text? To what extent do we struggle with some of the same issues?

Second, are we prepared to see, on the one hand how Jewish, how of its period and milieu is this most talked about yet most unread book? And on the other hand, are we prepared to take seriously a document which is challenging, questioning, poetic, innovative, sometimes rooted in our own tradition sometimes not, yet inexorably taking Judaism in a new direction?

Third, are we prepared to concede that when all is said and done and when the New Testament text is understood in all its religious, historical and political complexities, what was emerging at that time were two different world-views, two different understandings of the role of the Jewish people, two different responses to the promptings of God? In other words, are we prepared to acknowledge that this was a period of choice – for instance, as Braybrooke expressly suggests, over the balance of universalism and particularism that should be adopted?

We complain, rightly, that the portrait of Christianity as coming to complete Judaism is arrogant, since Judaism neither needed or needs such completion. We complain bitterly, as I suggested earlier, that the portrayal of the debates between Jesus and the Pharisees as a never-ending round of humiliating defeats for pharisaic Judaism is a travesty – but are we prepared to acknowledge that in this period, perhaps inevitably, perhaps not, the ways were parting over genuine and honest disagreements and choices?

Which leads me to two final questions, perhaps the most difficult of all. The traditional Jewish shopping list widely shared by those prepared to engage in dialogue includes near the top of the list a demand that Christians retract the long-held view that the Jews have been replaced as the Children of Israel, the beloved of God, that they have been superseded, that the covenant at Sinai has been broken or rescinded. We are not keen on Christian supercessionism and bridle at the very terms *New* and *Old* Testament which reflect this unflattering theology. In recent years, a great deal of progress has been made in many sections of the Christian world and Marcus Braybrooke welcomes this and reflects this. However, there is a reciprocal question which is far less frequently voiced but ought to be voiced. If Christians acknowledge that the covenant at Sinai is unbroken and that the Hebrew Bible is a book of independent revelation for Jews, are Jews prepared to acknowledge that the New Testament plays a similar and parallel role for Christians? Is the covenant at Sinai paralleled by the covenant at Golgotha (or are they both sub-sets of the covenant with Abraham?). Jews have long, long seen Jesus as an insignificant and unimportant Jew whose death by crucifixion gave rise to an incomprehensible and mistaken theology involving incarnation, resurrection and a number of other impenetrable beliefs. Is it possible for us, without betraying our own faith and the path we chose at the partings of the ways, to acknowledge that in the New Testament, in the life and death that it portrays, is revelation? Is it also possible for us to begin to understand why, if indeed the New Testament is a book of revelation, God should have acted thus? After all, we are not prepared to accept that the death of Jesus represents a collective Jewish failure, yet the consequences of the birth of this new faith have been disastrous for Jewry for the last two thousand years. What on earth was God up to? Those are hugely difficult questions, yet I cannot help feeling that the faith, goodness and generosity of many Christians demands that we attempt to respond.

So to my final question. Marcus Braybrooke quietly suggests in the course of his text that two religions – Christianity and rabbinic Judaism – were born, roughly at the same time, in those turbulent decades in Jerusalem some two thousand years ago. I first became aware of this way of looking at the events of that time when I read a book by a Jewish scholar, Alan Segal, nearly fifteen years ago.[13] Segal describes Judaism and Christianity as twins and refers back to Jacob and Esau struggling for supremacy even in Rebecca's womb. I would quibble about twins and would prefer the metaphor of siblings. But what is important is to realize how shocking and disturbing this suggestion is for Jews. It is one thing to describe Christianity as a daughter religion, quite another as a sibling. For if we are siblings, both born after the completion of the Hebrew Bible, then everything that precedes our birth – the story of Abraham and Sarah (*Avraham Avinu*, Abraham *our* parent, we say) the Torah, the Five Books of Moses, *our* Book of Revelation, the accounts of the journeys of the Children of Israel, the history, the generations, the genealogy of our people, the story that unfolds in Judges and Kings, the burning message of the Prophets, our most cherished liturgy, the Book of Psalms – must be shared. Is that the implication of the sibling metaphor? Is that the implication of the partings of the ways? Are Jews required, in return for a renunciation of supercessionism, to regard themselves no longer as God's first love, but rather as the numerically far less successful child of God's first love – and not even one of two, but as just one of the three children of Abraham?[14]

I cannot tell you how difficult it has been to write these last sentences. But then, I suspect, some of the sentences which Marcus Braybrooke has penned were also difficult and challenging. I think I should also add that I am far from sure that I know the answers to many of the questions that I have asked over the preceding pages. But then, I come from a tradition which has often realized that the question is more important and more powerful than the answer. They are certainly questions which Christians as insightful and magnanimous as Braybrooke should not be afraid to ask of Jews. Isn't that central to the meaning of dialogue?

FOR FURTHER READING

The literature on this subject is enormous and there are references in the notes to a number of relevant books. Ones listed here would serve as introductions to some of the areas discussed in this book.

On the Historical Jesus

Borg, Marcus J., *Jesus in Contemporary Scholarship*, Trinity Press International 1994.

Crossan, John Dominic, *The Historical Jesus: The Life of a Mediterranean Jewish Peasant*, HarperCollins 1992.

Theissen, Gerd, and Merz, Annette, *The Historical Jesus: A Comprehensive Guide*, SCM Press 1998.

On First-Century Judaism

Grabbe, Lester L., *An Introduction to First-Century Judaism: Jewish Religion and History in the Second Temple Period*, T&T Clark 1996.

Sanders, E. P., *Paul and Palestinian Judaism* and *Jesus and Judaism*, SCM Press 1977 and 1985.

On Anti-Semitism

Cohn-Sherbok, Dan, *The Crucified Jew: Twenty Centuries of Anti-Semitism*, HarperCollins 1992.

Gager, John, *The Origins of Anti-Semitism: Attitudes Toward Judaism in Pagan and Christian Antiquity,* OUP 1983. Part IV, 'The Case of Paul' is a particularly useful introduction to the new way of thinking about Paul.

Keith, Graham, *Hated Without a Cause?*, Paternoster Press 1997.

Jewish Attitudes to Other Faiths

Cohn-Sherbok, Dan, *Judaism and Other Faiths,* St Martin's Press 1994.

Jewish–Christian Relations

Braybrooke, Marcus, *Time to Meet,* SCM Press 1990.
Fry, Helen P., *Christian–Jewish Dialogue,* University of Exeter Press 1996.

NOTES

1. The Present Plateau

1. David Rosen in an address to the International Council of Christians and Jews.
2. Some non-Orthodox congregations in the USA will recognize children of Jewish fathers as Jewish.
3. Jonathan Sacks, 'From Integration to Survival to Continuity: The Third Great Era of Modern Jewry' in *Jewish Identities in the New Europe*, ed. Jonathan Webber, Littman Library of Jewish Civilization 1994, p. 113. See also Jonathan Sacks, *Crisis and Covenant*, Manchester University Press 1992 and Norman Cantor, *The Sacred Chain*, HarperCollins 1995, esp. ch. 12.
4. Reported in the *Church Times*, 18.12.98, p. 1
5. See the back cover of *People of God, Peoples of God*, ed. Hans Ucko, World Council of Churches 1996.
6. Shaye J. D. Cohen, 'The Unfinished Agenda of Jewish–Christian Dialogue', *Journal of Ecumenical Studies*, Vol. 34, No. 3, Summer 1997, p. 326.
7. Cohen, 'Unfinished Agenda', p. 328.
8. Cohen, 'Unfinished Agenda', p. 327.
9. The fifteenth-century Council of Florence decreed that 'no one remaining outside the Catholic Church, not just pagans, but also Jews or heretics or schismatics, can become partakers of eternal life; but they will go to the "everlasting fire which was prepared for the devil and his angels", unless before the end of life they are joined to the Church' (*The Church Teaches: Documents of the Church in English Translation*, B. Herder Book Co. 1955, pp. 165f). See further John Hick, *God and the Universe of Faiths*, Macmillan 1973, pp. 120ff.
10. See Marcus Braybrooke, *Time to Meet*, SCM Press 1990, Part One.
11. Allan Brockway in *The Theology of the Churches and the Jewish People*, eds Allan Brockway, Paul van Buren, Rolf Rendtorff and Simon

Schoon, WCC Publications, Geneva 1988, p. 186.
12. Quoted in *Time to Meet*, p. 59.

2. *Looking Back*

1. See Marcus Braybrooke, *Children of One God*, Vallentine Mitchell 1991, p. 52.
2. Rosemary Radford Ruether in *The Holocaust Now*, ed. Steven Jacobs, Cummings and Hathaway 1996, p. 328.
3. See Graham Keith, *Hated Without a Cause?*, Paternoster Press 1997; Dan Cohn-Sherbok, *The Crucified Jew*, HarperCollins 1992.
4. In *Christian–Jewish Relations*, Institute of Jewish Affairs, Vol. 19, No. 3, June 1986, p. 3.
5. Ronald H. Miller, *Dialogue and Disagreement*, University Press of America 1989, p. 108.
6. F. Rosenzweig, *Briefe und Tagebücher*, I, 1, pp. 543–44, quoted and translated by Ronald Miller in *Dialogue and Disagreement*, p. 107.
7. See Braybrooke, *Children of One God*, pp. 4–5.
8. Quoted in Robert A. Everett, *Christianity Without Anti-Semitism: James Parkes and the Jewish Christian Encounter*, Pergamon Press 1993, p. 25.
9. See Marcus Braybrooke, *Pilgrimage of Hope*, SCM Press 1992, chs 19–23.
10. See *Immanuel* 26/27, 1994 (Journal of the Ecumenical Theological Research Fraternity, Jerusalem), issue devoted to 'Orthodox Christians and Jews on Continuity and Renewal'.

3. *The Jewish World at the Time of Jesus*

1. *The Common Bond – Christians and Jews: Notes for Preaching and Teaching*, Pontifical Commission for Religious Relations with the Jews, Rome, June 1985.
2. The emphasis on the Jewishness of Jesus was described fourteen years ago as 'a minor revolution in biblical studies with more far reaching consequences than is usually recognized' by Alastair Hunter of Glasgow University in 'Rite of Passage: The Implications of Matthew 4.1–11', *Christian–Jewish Relations*, Vol. 19, No. 4, December 1986, p. 8.
3. See, for example, James D. G. Dunn, *The Partings of the Ways*, SCM Press 1991.

4. See Denis Thomas, *The Face of Christ*, Hamlyn 1979 and Heinz Schreckenberg, *The Jews in Christian Art*, SCM Press 1996.

5. J. Wellhausen, *Einleitungin die ersetn drei Evangelien*, 2nd edn, Berlin 1911, p. 102.

6. Charles Wesley's 'Lo, he comes with clouds descending', 241 in *Hymns and Psalms*.

7. Dietrich Bonhoeffer, *Ethics*, ed. Eberhard Bethge, SCM Press 1955; Fontana edn 1964, pp. 90–91.

8. See, for example, Clark M. Williamson and Ronald J. Allen, *Interpreting Difficult Texts: Anti-Judaism and Christian Preaching*, SCM Press 1989.

9. Rabbi Michael Hilton and Fr Gordian Marshall, for example, in their joint study of *The Gospels and Rabbinic Judaism* (SCM Press 1988) say that the oral transmission of rabbinic ideas was very important and the rabbinic texts clearly reflect much earlier material.

10. Lester Grabbe in his *An Introduction to First Century Judaism*, T&T Clark 1996, p. 41, points out three difficulties with this assumption that rabbinic material can be assumed to tell us what the Pharisees taught: '(a) only a few passages refer to the *perushim*, a word usually taken to be the Hebrew origin of the term "Pharisees" which comes from Greek literature; (b) we have no evidence that most of the rabbis before 70 were Pharisees or that the bulk of the rabbinic literature was written by Pharisees; (c) much of the literature is centuries after 70 CE and is unlikely to have been written by Pharisees even if the latter continued to exist after 70.'

11. For a clear summary discussion about the reliability of Josephus and of other sources see Lester Grabbe, *Introduction to First Century Judaism* and Günther Sternberger, *Jewish Contemporaries of Jesus*, Fortress Press 1995.

12. See the Introduction to Geza Vermes' *The Dead Sea Scrolls in English*, Penguin 1962, 4th revd edn 1995 or James H. Charlesworth, *Jesus Within Judaism*, SPCK 1989, *passim*.

13. There is a good summary in Gerd Theissen and Annette Merz, *The Historical Jesus: A Comprehensive Guide*, SCM Press 1998.

14. John Bowker, *Jesus and the Pharisees*, CUP 1973, p. 32.

15. Marvin R. Wilson, *Our Father Abraham*, Eerdmans, Grand Rapids 1989, pp. 64–72.

16. See J. D. Crossan, *The Historical Jesus*, HarperSanFrancisco 1992, pp. xi–xxvi.

17. See Theissen and Merz, *The Historical Jesus*, pp. 139–40 for a sum-

mary of the discussion. Theissen refers to J. Neusner, *From Politics to Piety*, Prentice-Hall 1973; Martin Hengel, *The Zealots: Investigations Into Jewish Freedom Movements in the Period from Herod Until AD 70*, T&T Clark 1989 and E. P. Sanders, *Judaism*, SCM Press 1992. See also Grabbe, *Introduction to First-Century Judaism*, pp. 463–552.

18. John Bowker, *Jesus and the Pharisees*, p. 31.
19. *Jesus and the Pharisees*, p. 32.
20. K. Berger, 'Jesus als Pharisäer und frühe Christen als Pharisäer', *Novum Testamentum*, 30, 1988, pp. 231–62, quoted by Theissen and Merz, *The Historical Jesus*, p. 141.
21. See further in the next chapter.
22. Theissen and Merz, *The Historical Jesus*, p. 177.
23. Geza Vermes, *Jesus the Jew*, Collins 1973; 2nd edn SCM Press 1983, p. 54. See also Theissen and Merz, *The Historical Jesus*, p. 178.
24. Vermes, *Jesus the Jew*, p. 57; Theissen and Merz, *The Historical Jesus*, p. 176.
25. Hyam Maccoby in *Judaism in the First Century*, Sheldon Press 1989, p. 12, implies that the scribes were Pharisees. Theissen and Merz question this, *The Historical Jesus*, pp. 226–27.
26. Theissen and Merz, *The Historical Jesus*, p. 232. See Josephus, *Antiquities*, 13.408f. and 13.297f.
27. *Antiquities*, 20.200.
28. Grabbe, *Introduction to First Century Judaism*, p. 59.
29. *Antiquities*, 18.1.6, 23–25.
30. Grabbe, *Introduction to First Century Judaism*, p. 62.
31. The social, political and economic setting of Jesus' ministry is fully discussed by Crossan, *The Historical Jesus*. See also Theissen and Merz, *The Historical Jesus*, pp. 168–178.

4. *Jesus and the Judaism of His Day*

1. *The Times*, 3.2.2000, p. 22.
2. Robert W. Funk, *Honest to Jesus*, HarperCollins 1996, p. 58. In fairness to him, I should quote the rest of the paragraph: 'Used without qualification, "Jesus the Jew" often means Jesus spoke and behaved like all other Jews in his time and place. There are two things wrong with this assumption. First, we don't know as much as we would like about the religion of the Second Temple (*c.* 520 BCE to 70 CE) and especially about Jewish behaviour in semipagan Galilee. The temptation is to read rabbinic Judaism, which did not take shape until after

the fall of Jerusalem in 70 CE, back into Galilee in the first decades of the common era. That would be an anachronism. In the second place, Jesus was not just another Jew. John the Baptist was not just another Jew. Caiaphas was not just another Jew . . . Jesus must have been enough of an individual to have said and done some things that were unusual or at least distinctive.'

3. Quoted by Crossan in *The Historical Jesus*, p. xxvii.

4. Ibid.

5. For a survey of North-American contributions to the debate, see Marcus J. Borg, *Jesus in Contemporary Scholarship*, Trinity Press International 1994, ch. 2, pp. 18ff.

6. Torah originally meant an individual teaching given to a prophet or priest. It came to be used of the first five books of the Bible, the books of Moses, which have primary importance in Judaism. Torah is sometimes used to mean the whole Hebrew Bible and can be extended to include the writings that interpret the Bible or even to mean the whole corpus of Jewish religious literature and teaching. See further my *How to Understand Judaism*, SCM Press 1995, pp. 42–43.

7. E. Stauffer, *Die Botschaft Jesu*, Bern 1959, p. 26, quoted by Theissen and Merz, *The Historical Jesus*, p. 347.

8. Leonard Swidler, *Bursting the Bonds*, Orbis 1990, p. 57.

9. David Flusser, *Jesus in Selbstzeugnissen und Bilddokumenten*, Reinbeck 1968, p. 43.

10. Nicholas de Lange, 'Who is Jesus?', *SIDIC, 12, 3* (1979), p. 12.

11. *Hymns Ancient and Modern Revised*, 210.

12. *Methodist Hymn Book*, 1933, 350.

13. E. P. Sanders, *Paul and Palestinian Judaism*, SCM Press 1977, p. 59.

14. E. P. Sanders, *Jesus and Judaism*, SCM Press 1985, p. 336.

15. Pinchas Lapide, *Er predigte in ihren Synogogen*, Gerd Mohn, Gütersloh 1980, p. 30. Quoted by Swidler, *Bursting the Bonds* (n.8) p. 75

16. J. C. Fenton, *Saint Matthew*, Penguin 1963, p. 18.

17. Theissen and Merz, *The Historical Jesus*, pp. 342–43.

18. See M. Smith, *Jesus the Magician*, Harper and Row 1978.

19. Geza Vermes compares Jesus to Honi and Hanina ben Dosa. They renounced possessions and were indifferent to questions of ritual. They were active through prayer – it was God who performed the miracles, not they themselves. See *Jesus the Jew*, pp. 58–82.

20. Theudas, for example, promised to repeat the miracle of the crossing of the Jordan and Acts 21.38 refers to the Egyptian rebel leader.

21. Theissen and Merz, *The Historical Jesus*, p. 309.
22. Crossan, *The Historical Jesus*, pp. 301–53.
23. Theissen and Merz, *The Historical Jesus*, p. 221.
24. See Sanders, *Jesus and Judaism*, pp. 245ff. In my *Time to Meet*, p. 56, this was the position, following Sanders, that I adopted.
25. Borg, *Jesus in Contemporary Scholarship*, pp. 69–96.
26. *Jesus in Contemporary Scholarship*, p. 275.
27. K. Berger, *Die Gesetzesauslegung Jesu I*, Wissenschaftliche Monographien zum Alten und Neuen Testament 40, Neukirchen 1972, p. 39.
28. Theissen and Merz, *The Historical Jesus*, p. 381.
29. This section is based primarily on ch. 5 of Marcus Borg's *Jesus in Contemporary Scholarship*, but see also his major works, *Conflict, Holiness and Politics in the Teaching of Jesus*, Edwin Mellen Press 1984 and *Jesus: A New Vision*, HarperSanFrancisco 1987 and *Meeting Jesus Again for the First Time*, HarperSanFrancisco 1994.
30. Borg, *Jesus in Contemporary Scholarship*, p. 115.
31. Crossan, *The Historical Jesus*, pp. 421–42.
32. Crossan, *The Historical Jesus*, p. 423.

5. *The Death of Jesus*

1. Martin Gilbert, *The Holocaust*, Collins 1986, p. 19.
2. Robert Runcie, 'Kristallnacht Address' in *Common Ground*, CCJ, London 1989, No.1.
3. See Marc Sapperstein, *Moments of Crisis in Jewish–Christian Relations*, SCM Press 1989, pp. 38ff.
4. Quoted from the National Section of the *New York Times*, 27.3.1994, in John Dominic Crossan, *Who Killed Jesus?* HarperSanFrancisco 1996, p. 1.
5. Simon Légasse, *The Trial of Jesus*, SCM Press 1997, pp. vii–viii.
6. Philo, *Legatio ad Gaium*, 302–3, quoted by Légasse, *The Trial of Jesus*, p. 140.
7. Paul Winter, *On the Trial of Jesus*, Berlin 1961; revd edn Berlin and New York 1974.
8. jSanh 1.18a; 7.24b.
9. BJ 5, 193; 6, 124–6.
10. Légasse, *The Trial of Jesus*, p. 53.
11. See Theissen and Merz, *The Historical Jesus*, pp. 457–58 and Légasse, *The Trial of Jesus*, p. 63.

12. Mark 13.2 = Matt. 24.2 and Luke 21.6; Mark 14.58 = Matt. 26.21; John 2.19.
13. See Légasse, *The Trial of Jesus*, p. 30; Sanders, *Jesus and Judaism*, p. 85 and my *Time to Meet*, pp. 55–56.
14. *Antiquities*, 13.79.
15. Detailed references to the Jewish sources are given by Theissen and Merz, *The Historical Jesus*, ch. 14 and esp. pp. 455–66.
16. Justin, *Dial*. 69. 7; 108. 2; cf. Mark 3.20–30.
17. Légasse, *The Trial of Jesus*, pp. 37–38.
18. J. Blinzler, *The Trial of Jesus*, Westminster, Maryland 1959.
19. H. Lietzmann, 'Der Prozess Jesu' (1931) in *Kleine Schriften II*, Berlin 1958. See also Winter, *On the Trial of Jesus*.
20. Sanhedrin IV, 1 etc.
21. This is based on material in Theissen and Merz, *The Historical Jesus*, p. 461.
22. Raymond Brown, *The Death of the Messiah*, 2 vols with continuous pagination, Anchor Bible Reference Library, Doubleday, New York 1994, pp. 362f.
23. *The Death of the Messiah*, p. 345.
24. Légasse, *The Trial of Jesus*, pp. 39–50.
25. Crossan, *Who Killed Jesus?*, p. 158; Brown, *The Death of the Messiah*, p. 833.
26. Brown, *The Death of the Messiah*, p. 29.
27. Williamson and Allen, *Interpreting Difficult Texts*, p. 88.
28. Ellis Rivkin, *What Crucified Jesus*, SCM Press 1984, p. 117, quoted by Williamson and Allen, *Interpreting Difficult Texts*, p. 86.

6. The Resurrection

1. Alice L. Eckardt and A. Roy Eckardt, *Long Night's Journey Into Day*, Wayne State University Press, Detroit 1982; revd edn 1988, pp. 140–41.
2. John Pawlikowski, *Christ in the Light of Jewish–Christian Dialogue*, Paulist Press 1982, pp. 114–55.
3. See Pinchas Lapide, *The Resurrection of Jesus*, SPCK 1984.
4. See further R. H. Lightfoot, *The Gospel Message of St Mark*, OUP 1950; 1962 edn, pp. 80–97.
5. Rowan Williams, *Resurrection*, Darton, Longman and Todd 1982.
6. See some of the views summarized by Lapide, *The Resurrection of Jesus*, pp. 128–29.

7. *Lent, Holy Week, Easter: Services and Prayers*, Church House Publishing/ CUP/ SPCK 1984, p. 231.
8. Office Hymn in *English Hymnal*, 123.
9. Office Hymn in *English Hymnal*, 122.
10. 'The strife is o'er' in *Hymns Ancient and Modern Revised*, 135.
11. See *Youth Praise*, 32.
12. Irenaeus, *Adv. Haer.* IV, 41, 2., quoted by Gustaf Aulén, *Christus Victor*, SPCK 1961, p. 42.
13. See further *Dialogue with a Difference*, eds Tony Bayfield and Marcus Braybrooke, SCM Press 1992, pp. 81–93.
14. Rosemary Radford Ruether, 'Old Problems and New Dimensions' in *Anti-Semitism and the Foundations of Christianity*, ed. Alan T. Davies, Paulist Press 1979, p. 251.
15. Irving Greenberg, 'Theological Reflections on the Holocaust' in *Auschwitz: Beginning of a New Era?* ed. Eva Fleischner, Ktav 1977, pp. 27–28.
16. Quoted by Lapide, *The Resurrection of Jesus*, p. 91.

7. 'He Humbled Himself'

1. From a Collect for Good Friday in *The Book of Common Prayer*.
2. The reference is to Phil. 2.4–11 which, besides speaking of Christ's humanity, also says that to him every knee should bow. Reference is also made to the Good Friday Collect and a prayer for the sovereign in *The Book of Common Prayer*.
3. See, e.g., the hymn 'Majesty' by Jack W. Hayford, in *Junior Praise*, 160.
4. Gerd Lüdemann, *What Really Happened to Jesus*, SCM Press 1995, p. 136.
5. Desmond Tutu, *No Future Without Forgiveness*, Rider 1999, p. 75.
6. Samuel Crossman (1624–83), 'My song is love unknown' in *Hymns and Psalms*, 173.
7. See further Bayfield and Braybrooke, *Dialogue with a Difference*, p. 84 and *Glimpses of God*, ed. Dan Cohn-Sherbok, Duckworth 1994, pp. 74–76.
8. Raymond Brown, 'Does the New Testament Call Jesus God?', *Theological Studies*, 26, No. 4, December 1965, p. 546.
9. See for example the very different ways in which artists through the centuries have pictured Jesus. Examples are given by Denis Thomas in *The Face of Christ*, Hamlyn 1979.

10. See my *Time to Meet*, ch. 5, pp. 59–71 and Dunn, *The Partings of the Ways*, chs 9 and 10, pp. 163–206.

11. See Dunn, *The Partings of the Ways*, pp. 171–74 and Borg, *Jesus in Contemporary Scholarship*, pp. 51–53.

12. See Dunn, *The Partings of the Ways*, p. 169. For a different view, see Bruce Chilton, *Jewish and Christian Doctrines*, eds Jacob Neusner and Bruce Chilton, Routledge 2000, p. 54.

13. See further David Novak, *Jewish–Christian Dialogue: A Jewish Justification*, OUP 1989, pp. 57–72.

14. Ninian Smart, 'Empiricism and Religions' in *Essays in Philosophy Presented to Dr T. M. P. Mahadevan*, Ganesh, Madras 1962, p. 189.

15. See further Wilfred Cantwell Smith, *What is Scripture?*, SCM Press 1993, p. 11.

16. The technical word is hypostatized. See further Dunn, *The Partings of the Ways*, pp. 207–29 and L. W. Hurtado, *One God, One Lord*, SCM Press 1988.

17. Jacobus Schoneveld, 'The Jewish "No" to Jesus and the Christian "Yes" to Jews', *Quarterly Review*, 4, 1984, p. 60, quoted by Eckardt, *Long Night's Journey Into Day*, pp. 140–1.

18. Lapide, *The Resurrection of Jesus*, p. 135. See also Michael E. Lodahl, 'Christo-Praxis: Foundations for a Post-Holocaust Ethical Christology' in *Journal of Ecumenical Studies*, Vol. 30, No. 2, Spring 1993.

19. Alan F. Segal, 'Outlining the Question: From Christ to God' in *Jews and Christians Speak of Jesus*, ed. Arthur E. Zannoni, Fortress Press 1994, p. 131.

20. Dunn, *The Partings of the Ways*, p. 191.

21. *The Partings of the Ways*, p. 199.

22. Segal, 'Outlining the Question', pp. 131–32.

23. Dunn, *The Partings of the Ways*, p. 229 (his italics).

24. *The Partings of the Ways*, p. 282.

25. Monika Hellwig, 'From Christ to God: The Christian Perspective' in *Jews and Christians Speak of Jesus*, p. 139.

26. From the opening greeting of Ignatius' *Letter to the Romans*, ET in Henry Bettenson, *The Early Christian Fathers*, OUP 1956, p. 61.

27. From Ignatius' letters to the Romans and the Ephesians, quoted by J. N. D. Kelly, *Early Christian Doctrines*, A&C Black, 2nd edn 1960, p. 143.

28. Justin, *Dial.* 87, 2; cf. *I Apol.* 46, 5.

29. Hellwig, 'From Christ to God', p. 139. The reference is to Athenagoras,

Plea for Christians, ET J. H. Creham, Newman, New York 1956, ch. 10.1 ff.

30. Origen, *De Principiis* 2, 6.2.
31. See Kelly, *Early Christian Doctrines*, p. 155.
32. Hellwig, 'From Christ to God', p. 142.
33. See, e.g., *The Myth of God Incarnate*, ed. John Hick, SCM Press 1977.
34. Gregory Baum, 'Catholic Dogma After Auschwitz' in *Anti-Semitism and the Foundations of Christianity*, ed. Alan T. Davies, Paulist Press, New York 1979, p. 145.
35. Hellwig, 'From Christ to God', p. 142.
36. 'From Christ to God', pp. 142–43.
37. Pawlikowski, *Christ in the Light of Christian–Jewish Dialogue*, p. 10.
38. In Hick, *The Myth of God Incarnate*, p. 178.

8. Paul

1. So Lester Dean in *Bursting the Bonds*, p. 126.
2. Sanders, *Paul and Palestinian Judaism*, p. 1.
3. N. T. Wright, *The Climax of the Covenant*, T&T Clark 1991, pp. 173–74.
4. Martin Luther, *Luther's Works*, ed. J. Pelikan, Concordia, St Louis 1963–64, Vol. 26, p. 106. In this discussion of Luther, I rely primarily on the summary of his teaching by Stephen Westerholm in *Israel's Law and the Church's Faith*, Eerdmans, Grand Rapids 1988, pp. 1–12.
5. *Luther's Works*, Vol. 26, pp. 253–54.
6. *Luther's Works*, Vol. 26, p. 222.
7. *Luther's Works*, Vol. 27, p. 13.
8. W. G. Kümmel, *Römer 7 und das Bild des Menschen im Neuen Testament*, Christian Kaiser, Munich 1974. See also Westerholm, *Israel's Law and the Church's Faith*, pp. 52–65.
9. See for example Hendrik Kraemer, *Religion and the Christian Faith*, Lutterworth Press 1956.
10. *Hymns and Psalms*, 697 and 273, and many other collections.
11. R. Bultmann, *Theology of the New Testament*, SCM Press 1952, Vol. I, pp. 279–80. See also Günther Bornkamm, *Paul*, Hodder and Stoughton 1975 edn, pp. 135, 143 and E. Käsemann, *Commentary on Romans*, Eerdmans, Grand Rapids 1980, p. 103.
12. See above, Chapter 4 *passim*, especially pp. 33–5, 82f.
13. Sanders, *Paul and Palestinian Judaism*, p. 145.
14. S. Schechter, *Aspects of Rabbinic Theology* (1909), Schocken 1961,

p. 117, quoted by Westerholm, *Israel's Law and the Church's Faith,* p. 136.

15. C. G. Montefiore, *Judaism and St Paul: Two Essays,* London 1914, p. 74, quoted by Sanders, *Paul and Palestinian Judaism,* p. 5

16. Montefiore, quoted by Sanders, *Paul and Palestinian Judaism.*

17. H. J. Schoeps, *Paul,* Lutterworth Press 1961, p. 213.

18. G. F. Moore, *Judaism in the First Centuries of the Christian Era: The Age of the Tannaim,* 3 vols, Cambridge, Mass. 1927–30, Vol. III, p. 151.

19. James Parkes, *Jesus, Paul and the Jews,* SCM Press 1936, p. 120.

20. Sanders, *Paul and Palestinian Judaism,* p. 422, described Judaism as 'covenantal nomism', which had eight key components:
    (1) God has chosen Israel;
    (2) God has given Israel the Law;
    (3) The Law implies God's promise to maintain that election;
    (4) The Law also implies the requirement to obey;
    (5) God rewards obedience and punishes transgression;
    (6) The Law provides for means of atonement;
    (7) Atonement results in maintenance or re-establishment of the covenantal relationship;
    (8) All those who are maintained in the covenant by obedience, atonement and God's mercy belong to the group which will be saved.

21. Sanders, *Paul and Palestinian Judaism,* p. 552 (author's italics).

22. Sanders, *Paul and Palestinian Judaism,* p. 551 (author's italics).

23. W. D. Davies, *Paul and Rabbinic Judaism* (1948), SPCK 1962, p. 324.

24. Lloyd Gaston, *Paul and Torah,* University of British Columbia Press, Vancouver 1987, p. 67 says: 'Paul's major theological concern I understand to be not the justification of individuals by their faith but the justification of the legitimacy of his apostleship to and gospel for the Gentiles.'

25. A. Schweitzer, *The Mysticism of Paul the Apostle,* Seabury Press, New York 1931, p. 220, says that the doctrine of righteousness by faith was 'not independent, but is worked out with the aid of conceptions drawn from the eschatological doctrine of the being-in-Christ.'

26. Schweitzer, *The Mysticism of Paul,* p. 26.

27. According to Sanders, *Jesus and Judaism,* p. 214, there were within the biblical prophets six, sometimes overlapping, expectations about the fate of the Gentiles at the end time.
    1. The wealth of the Gentiles will flow into Jerusalem (Isa. 45.14; cf. Isa. 60.5–16, 61.6; Micah 4.13; Zeph. 2.9; Tobit 13.11; I QM 12.13f.).
    2. The kings of the Gentiles will bow down and the Gentile nations

will serve Israel (Isa. 49.23; cf. 45.14; Micah 7.17 (lick the dust); I Enoch 90.30; I QM 12.13f. (quoting Isa. 49.23).

3. Israel will be a light to the nations; her salvation will go forth to the ends of the earth (Isa. 49.6; cf. Isa. 51.4; Isa. 2.2f.; Micah 4.1). It accords with this that the Gentiles may be added to Israel and thus be saved (Isa. 56.6–8; Zech. 2.11; 8.20–23; Isa. 45.22; Tobit 14.6 f.; I Enoch 90.30–33). Here we should include also the one passage which predicts a mission *to* the Gentiles (Isa. 66.19).

4. The Gentiles will be destroyed. Their cities will be desolate and will be occupied by Israel (Isa. 54.3; cf. Ecclus. 36.7; I Enoch 91.9, Baruch 4.25, 31, 35; I QM 12.10).

5. As a supplement to the theme of destruction we may add predictions of vengeance and the defeat of the Gentiles (Micah 5.10–15; Zeph. 2.10f.; T. Mos. 10, 7; Jub. 23.30; Ps. Sol. 17.25–27).

6. Foreigners will survive but will not dwell with Israel (Joel 3.17; Ps. Sol. 17.31.

28.   Matt. 23.15. Many of Paul's converts were 'God-fearers', Gentiles who attended the synagogue.

29.   Sanders, *Paul and Palestinian Judaism*, p. 217.

30.   Krister Stendahl, *Paul Among Jews and Gentiles,* SCM Press 1976, p. 87.

31.   John G. Gager, *The Origins of Anti-Semitism*, OUP 1983, pp. 200–1. See also Gaston, *Paul and the Torah.*

32.   Jubilees 15, 26, quoted by Francis Watson, *Paul, Judaism and the Gentiles,* CUP 1986; 1989 edn, p. 37. It may be that Paul's opponents, whom he criticizes, shared the views of those who spoke of an eternal Law or Torah. In the book of Jubilees and the Testaments of the Twelve Patriarchs there were attempts to retroject specific Torah observances into an earlier period, such as claiming that Abraham observed the Sabbath. These writings claimed that Torah had existed before the creation of the world and had been followed by Adam and Eve, by Noah, by Abraham and Sarah and by other patriarchs and matriarchs. Paul also seems to suggest that whereas the promise to Abraham was given directly by God, the Law was given to Israel by a mediator, namely Moses. The Law was given by an intermediary and not directly (Gal. 3. 19).

33.   Lester Dean in *Bursting the Bonds*, p. 149.

34.   Dean, *Bursting the Bonds*, p. 138.

35.   Gager, *The Origins of Anti-Semitism,* p. 214.

36.   See above, p. 83

9. An Enduring Covenant

1. Watson, *Paul, Judaism and the Gentiles*, pp. 28–38.
2. Alan F. Segal, *Paul the Convert*, Yale University Press 1990, p. 239.
3. Justin Martyr, *Dialogue with Trypho* 47, 1–4. The American scholar Terrence Callan, in his book *Forgetting the Root*, Paulist Press 1986, argues that it was the decision by the church that Gentiles need not keep the Jewish Law which led to the emergence of Christianity as a separate religion. He suggests that three positions can be discerned in the early church:
   1. There were conservative Jewish Christians who insisted that Gentile converts should observe the Law.
   2. There were liberal Jewish Christians who retained a positive view of Judaism, but did not hold that Gentile Christians were required to keep the Law.
   3. There were Gentile Christians who agreed that Gentiles need not keep the Law. This latter group soon lost sight of the positive place of Judaism in the economy of salvation. They came to a negative view of the Law and held that Jewish Christians and indeed Jews themselves should not observe it.
4. H. Räisänen, *Paul and the Law*, Fortress Press 1983; 1986 edn. See the summary in Westerholm, *Israel's Law and the Church's Faith*, pp. 94–95.
5. Sanders, *Paul and Palestinian Judaism*, p. 551.
6. Wright, *The Climax of the Covenant*, p. 54.
7. Wright, *The Climax of the Covenant*, p. 163.
8. Wright, *The Climax of the Covenant*, p. 173.
9. Stendahl, *Paul Among Jews and Gentiles*, p. 4. See also Gaston, *Paul and the Torah*, esp. pp. 135–50.
10. Jonathan Sacks, *The Persistence of Faith*, Weidenfeld and Nicolson 1991, p. 81.
11. Rabbi Rodney Mariner, 'A Jewish Response to Christian Missionary Activity', an unpublished paper given to the CCJ Missionary Advisory Committee, p. 1. See Marcus Braybrooke, *Time to Meet*, SCM Press 1990, p. 96.
12. Norman Solomon, *Judaism and World Religions*, Macmillan 1991, p. 233. See also Dan Cohn-Sherbok, *Judaism and Other Faiths*, St Martin's Press 1994.

13. Edwina Currie, *She's Leaving Home*, Little, Brown and Co. 1997, p. 411.
14. See, for example, Hugh Montefiore, *On Being a Jewish Christian*, Hodder and Stoughton 1998. The testimonies of some Messianic Jews are recorded by John Fieldsend in *Messianic Jews*, Monarch Publications 1993.
15. 'Jews, Christians and Muslims: The Way of Dialogue' in *The Truth Shall Make You Free. The Lambeth Conference 1988*, Anglican Consultative Council 1989. Appendix, p. 305. See also *More Stepping Stones to Jewish Christian Relations*, ed. Helga Croner, Stimulus Books 1985, p. 211.
16. Keith, *Hated Without a Cause?*, p. 73. The reference is to Baruch Maoz, 'Ethics in Jewish Evangelism', *Mishkan*, 19, 1993, p. 4.
17. See my *Time to Meet*, ch. 8.
18. *Time to Meet*, ch. 6.
19. Paul M. van Buren, *Discerning the Way*, Seabury Press 1980, p. 42.
20. In an address at a conference in Israel in 1994.
21. See above, pp. 7–8
22. Radford Ruether, *The Holocaust Now*, pp. 346–47. See also Choan-Seng Song, *The Compassionate God*, SCM Press 1982.
23. Radford Ruether, *The Holocaust Now*, p. 347.

10. *The Path Ahead*

1. 'Jews and Christians in Search of a Common Religious Basis for Contributing Towards a Better World', statement by the International Council of Christians and Jews in *Current Dialogue*, World Council of Churches, Geneva, No. 28, June 1995, pp. 11–15.
2. Donald Coggan, 'A Joint Trusteeship', *Common Ground*, CCJ, 1993, 1, pp. 4–5. See also Novak, *Jewish–Christian Dialogue*, esp. p. 156.
3. Ewert Cousins, 'Judaism-Christianity-Islam: Facing Modernity Together' in *Journal of Ecumenical Studies*, Summer/Fall 1993, Vol. 30, Nos 3–4, p. 425.
4. See note 1.

5. Arranged by the Center for Christian–Jewish Understanding of Sacred Heart University, 5151 Park Ave, Fairfield, Connecticut, 06432–1000, USA.
6. *A Global Ethic*, eds Hans Küng and Karl-Josef Kuschel, SCM Press 1993; 'A Call to the Guiding Institutions', Council for a Parliament of the World's Religions, PO Box 1630, Chicago, IL 60690–1630, USA. See also Marcus Braybrooke, *Faith and Interfaith in a Global Age*, CoNexus Press 1998.
7. *Commitment to Global Peace*, 31.8.2000, Document of the Millennium World Peace Summit, 301 East 57th Street, 3rd Floor, New York, NY 10022, USA.

Response

1. Philip Roth, *Portnoy's Complaint*, Jonathan Cape 1969, p. 111.
2. John 8.44.
3. Lionel Blue, *To Heaven with Scribes and Pharisees*, Darton Longman & Todd 1975.
4. Freiderich Heer, *God's First Love*, Weidenfeld & Nicolson, 1970.
5. The term refers to a book I have always found extremely helpful: Dunn, *The Partings of the Ways*.
6. Cf. Hans Küng, *Global Responsibility*, SCM Press 1991.
7. See *World Faith Encounter*, No. 26, July 2000.
8. Ibid.
9. Eliezer Berkovits, *Faith After the Holocaust*, Ktav, New York 1973, p. 47.
10. Joseph B. Soloveitchik, 'Confrontation', *Tradition*, 6, 2, Spring/Summer 1964, pp. 23–24.
11. See Jonathan Sacks, *L'Eylah Journal*, No. 21, pp. 41–47 and No. 26, pp. 13–19.
12. John Bowden, *Jesus: The Unanswered Questions*, SCM Press 1988.
13. Alan F. Segal, *Rebecca's Children: Judaism and Christianity in the Roman World*, Harvard University Press, Cambridge, Ma. 1986.
14. The third being Islam, born some centuries later.

INDEX OF NAMES